RUSSIAN GRAPHIC DESIGN 1880-1917

The rich holdings of the Lenin State Library of the U.S.S.R. include a particularly significant collection of Russian graphic design of the prerevolutionary era. During a trip to Moscow in 1988, I visited the Lenin Library at the recommendation of Bob Abrams, publisher of Abbeville Press. I was overwhelmed by the power and diversity of the works in the collection; at the same time I was struck by how unknown this material is in the West. Now, with the publication of *Russian Graphic Design: 1880–1917*, hundreds of works from this intensely creative period can finally be seen for the first time in many decades. The preparations for this book led to an opportunity for the American Federation of Arts to work with the Soviet Ministry of Culture and the Lenin State Library in organizing a traveling exhibition drawn from this remarkable collection. We gratefully acknowledge the assistance of these organizations as well as that of John Calmann & King Ltd and Abbeville Press.

Myrna Smoot
Director
American Federation of Arts

RUSSIAN GRAPHIC .DESIGN.

TEXT BY ELENA CHERNEVICH
COMPILED BY MIKHAIL ANIKST & NINA BABURINA
DESIGNED BY MIKHAIL ANIKST

1880 · 1917

ABBEVILLE PRESS · PUBLISHERS · NEW YORK

Library of Congress Cataloging-in-Publication Data

Chernevich, Elena, 1939–
    Russian graphic design
    1. Commercial art—Russian S.F.S.R.—History—19th century.
2. Graphic arts—Russian S.F.S.R.—History—19th century.
3. Book design—Russian S.F.S.R.—History—19th century.
I. Anikst, Mikhail. II. Baburina, N.I. (Nina Ivanovna). III. Title.
NC998.6.R9C47 1990   741.6′0947   90–248
ISBN 1–55859–016–1

Designed by Mikhail Anikst
Typeset by Black Box Ltd.
Printed and bound in Singapore by Toppan Ltd.

First edition

6

INTRODUCTION

14

CHAPTER ONE: THE STYLE RUSSE

38

CHAPTER TWO: THE *MODERNE*: RUSSIAN ART NOUVEAU

64

CHAPTER THREE: THE WORLD OF ART GROUP

86

CHAPTER FOUR: COMMERCIAL GRAPHICS

138

CHAPTER FIVE: POLITICAL GRAPHICS

158

NOTES

159

INDEX

The period covered by this book was one of great achievement. It was only after the abolition of serfdom in 1861 that Russia embarked on the phase of capitalist development of which Western European countries already had long experience. Russia was a country in a hurry. Both the society and the economy were obliged to develop at a much faster rate, and industrial production consequently became much more concentrated and intense, than had been the case in the West. The result was a healthy trade surplus; indeed, exports continued to exceed imports until shortly before the beginning of the First World War.

Railway construction was given priority in the new scheme of things. In 1861, no more than 1,488 versts (1,577 km or 985 miles) of permanent track – about twice the distance from Moscow to St. Petersburg – had been laid throughout the whole of the Empire, yet within the next few decades nearly all the main centres of the country were to become accessible by rail.

In the last decade of the nineteenth century alone, foreign investment in Russian industry and banking (largely from Germany) increased four- or five-fold. A typical example was the opening in St. Petersburg of a branch of the Berlin-based firm of Berthold, which, together with the Russian firm of Leman, monopolized the design and production of typesetting equipment. Printing firms, like the rest of industry, underwent a technical revolution and were re-equipped with the latest machinery. As early as 1903, the journal *World of Art,* reporting the colour reproduction of a watercolour by Konstantin Somov on the cover of the German magazine *Kunst und Künstler,* remarked proudly that it had been printed to a higher standard in Russia than it would have been in Germany, the world capital of printing technology.

A building boom in the major towns and cities produced a multitude of new apartments for rent, banks and factories. Moscow, in particular, was transformed, becoming in the process the capital of the burgeoning merchant class. Once dismissed as a 'big village', the city now acquired a new nickname, 'the Russian Manchester'.

The balance of social forces altered drastically in the course of a single generation. The dominant position was now occupied by a new class, the industrial bourgeoisie, the majority of whose most powerful members were descended from serfs. Many of these men became famous not only for their business acumen and their millions but for their contribution to national culture. Sergei Morozov financed the Moscow Art Theatre; the school organized by Alexei Prokhorov for his factory workers was considered the best in Moscow, and he was made a member of the French Legion d'Honneur for his caring approach to his workers.

Private patronage of the arts was an indispensable element of late nineteenth-century Russian culture; but the patrons were now merchants and industrialists rather than, as before, members of the nobility and higher aristocracy. In 1892 one prominent industrialist, Pavel Tretyakov, donated his collection of Russian art to Moscow, thereby founding one of the most important of all national

One of the main shopping streets in Moscow – most of the shops are textile retailers. In the background is the Spassky Tower of the Kremlin.

collections, the Tretyakov Gallery. Russia's first theatre museum was opened with the financial backing of Alexei Bakhrushin. More than 300 museums of the most varied kinds sprang up in Russia in the decades preceding the First World War, the majority based on private collections. Two Moscow patrons, Sergei Shchukin and Ivan Morozov, assembled unique collections of new Western art. Shchukin's gallery, which was open to the public on Sundays, exerted an enormous influence on the development of young artists at the turn of the century; his Gauguins, Matisses, Picassos and other paintings became a kind of 'radical academy of art' (as a contemporary described it) for the future artists of the Russian avant-garde.

'One man', said Konstantin Stanislavsky, '. . . stood out among all the contributors to Russian cultural life for his talent, versatility and wide-ranging energy. This was the famous Savva Ivanovich Mamontov. He was a singer, operatic performer, director and playwright, as well as the creator of a private Russian opera. He was as important a patron of painting as Tretyakov – and responsible, what is more, for the construction of numerous railway lines.'[1]

In the 1880s and 1890s, the Russian intelligentsia, acutely aware of its obligations to the people, turned its attention to furthering popular education. Free schools, open on Sundays, were instituted, together with public libraries and reading-rooms. Societies for the encouragement of literacy sprang up, to enable the educated section of society to teach the unlettered. This programme of public education was a vivid and typical expression of the spirit of the times.

The growth in literacy brought in its wake a demand for books; and publishing expanded in step with educational activity. Few books had been produced in feudal Russia, for the educated classes generally preferred foreign literature. Now, however, publishing houses began to proliferate; in 1860 a mere two thousand titles had been published in Russia, but by 1887 the annual total had increased to 8,700 and in 1904 it reached 15,800.

Priority was given to the needs of the newly literate, a policy which resulted in the mass production of elementary textbooks, prayer-books, calendars, works of reference and pamphlets of every conceivable kind. The most important Russian publisher of such literature was Ivan Sytin, whose publishing house was to become the largest in Russia by the time of the First World War. In 1901, the journal *The Art of Printing* commented: 'Some idea of the vast circulation of I. D. Sytin's publications may be gained from the fact that his product sold at this year's trade fair amounted to approximately 20,000 poods [over 300 tons].'[2]

One particularly striking aspect of all this publishing activity was the rapid growth of new periodicals and newspapers, both in the capital and in the provinces. By the end of the century, light illustrated magazines 'for family reading' were the staple mental diet of the majority of the literate population. The most popular of these magazines was *Niva,* produced by Adolf Marx, a powerful businessman and an innovative publisher. He conceived the idea of rewarding annual subscribers to the magazine with a free edition of the collected works of one or other of the giants of Russian literature. Consequently, the circulation of *Niva* soared, and ordinary people throughout the Empire began to read Russian literature to an unprecedented extent.

We are bound to view the graphic design of a century or so ago from the perspective of our own

Right: one of the Art Nouveau buildings – in this case a manufactory, although many were offices – that sprang up at the turn of the century in old Moscow. Around it are some of the oldest buildings in the city.

Opposite: a Moscow shopping thoroughfare. On the left is St. Basil's Cathedral, and the battlements of the Kremlin's outer wall can just be glimpsed in the background.

day; clearly, therefore, our responses to it will not always coincide with those of the public for whom it was originally intended. Some features, not remarkable at the time simply because they were part of everyday life, strike us as especially interesting. For example, we learn that there was a whole separate graphic genre devoted to the large, lavishly decorated menus displayed on the walls of restaurants; we are even more intrigued to read what was actually served for dinner on, say, 15 May 1896. It is fascinating to discover not only the splendid posters of the *moderne* style (the term usually employed to designate Russian Art Nouveau), which were quite as fine as the best Western European examples, but also the designs for the ephemera of the time, such as the numerous profiles of women on chocolate wrappers, tins of powder and boxes of soap.. The exquisite calligraphic quality of the typefaces and colour lithography was commonplace at the time but is hardly to be found today.

Posters were an important element of Russian graphic design. In 1897, at the first International Exhibition of Art Posters in St. Petersburg, Russian posters still seemed rather unremarkable compared with the well-known works of such artists as Jules Chéret, Henri de Toulouse-Lautrec, Alphonse Mucha, Théophile Steinlein or Thomas Heine. The Russian representation at the exhibition was modest: out of more than seven hundred works, only twenty-eight were by Russian artists. Nevertheless, in the last years of the nineteenth century and for years thereafter, Russian poster design went from strength to strength and attracted some of the country's best artists.

The increasing respect paid to graphic design in the first decade of the twentieth century is instanced by the fact that when the All-Russian Congress of Artists opened at the end of 1911 it was marked by two exhibitions: one was of icons, and the other was devoted to 'Book and Poster Art'. The

range of the latter show was very broad; the catalogue included book illustration and decoration, caricature, posters, postcards, bookplates and etchings. This juxtaposition of the ancient art of icon-painting with an entirely contemporary art which used print as a means of expression is highly characteristic of the culture of the time.

Among the sources of the emergence of Russian graphic design was a quite new branch of the arts, that of industrial design, which began to develop both in theory and in practice at the end of the nineteenth century. It sprang from a recognition of the need to forge a link between art and the ornamental forms of industrially produced objects. The early twentieth-century industrial design movement, which was intimately related to Russian graphic design as a whole, is the direct antecedent of modern work in this field.

The year 1898 saw the almost simultaneous appearance of two new journals that were to become focal points of Russian artistic life for several years. These were *World of Art* and *Art and Industrial Design* – magazines of a new type, large in format and size, containing generous numbers of illustrations and reflecting a serious approach to all questions of design. For the first time, industrial design had acquired a published voice of its own, and a rank equal to fine art in general. Here was concrete evidence of public recognition of the importance of this new sphere of activity.

The new journals still contained very little material specifically concerned with the problems of

Above: Nevsky Prospekt, the busy and fashionable main boulevard of St. Petersburg. Slightly set back from the street is the Roman Catholic Church of St. Catherine, built in the mid-eighteenth century to the design of the architect Rinaldi.

Right: Singer sewing machines. This popular shop advertised widely; one of the posters that can just be seen on the billboards is reproduced on p.97.

graphic design (apart from the regular publication of book illustrations), although such design was already being applied widely in many spheres of everyday life. Nevertheless their general mood, a preoccupation with the fate of Russian art, together with critical reviews of all major national and international exhibitions, articles on Russian folk art and the history of architecture, and finally the constant presence of the very theme of industrial design – all these elements were bound to have an impact on the world of professional graphic designers.

As may be imagined, the presentation of the journals themselves was particularly influential, expecially that of *World of Art*, which was practically a design school in itself. Right from the start, its editors decided that its style and image should be an essential ingredient of the total concept of the magazine. Every aspect, including the typeface, paper and printing process appropriate to each particular illustration, was carefully considered; particular attention was paid to the selection and arrangement of the illustrations themselves and the design of the covers. This search for 'optimal solutions' continued throughout the magazine's existence.

We cannot but admire the large number of altruistic initiatives in the cause of national culture that were undertaken with great energy – and at their own expense – by the Russian intelligentsia of the day. Take, for example, an article carried by *Art and Industrial Design* in 1899, headed 'A New Branch of Industrial Design', which was intended to popularize 'artistic postcards'. The author, N. Shabelskaya, was introduced as 'a collector of objects of national art, dedicated to their reproduction for mass enjoyment'. She gave a detailed description of the uses of such cards, the lessons to be learnt from them, the opportunities they might offer to publishers and the subjects they might cover. She had formulated these ideas in the course of a two-year tour of Europe during which she had discovered this 'new branch of industrial design and art'. The article is redolent of her devotion to Russia, its people and its culture. Her purpose is summed up in its concluding words: 'The postcard, as a means of spreading knowledge and developing a sense of beauty and a love of nature, is not a frivolity. Effort expended on its design is highly important and fruitful, for it can do great service to the cause of popular education in the widest sense of the word. Artists working on postcards are toiling on behalf of the people. It is profoundly to be desired that Russian artists dedicate some part of their energies to this modest but richly rewarding art-form.'[3]

To judge by one announcement that appeared in *Art and Industrial Design* in that same year of 1899, the situation must have changed almost overnight: 'Postcards and other cards with drawings by, among others, Beggrov, Benois, Vasnetsov, Nesterov and Samokish, together with Red Cross envelopes

for greeting-cards and letters (good substitutes for actually paying visits) designed by Professor Sultanov and Academician Suslov for the benefit of the hospital and educational courses organized by the Community of St. Eugenia, may be purchased from the editorial offices of *Art and Industrial Design* (83, Moika Street) and at the exhibitions of the Imperial Society for the Encouragement of the Arts (38, Bolshaya Morskaya Street).'[4]

This undramatic announcement reveals several interesting facts. The artists named as involved in this new-born graphic field include such legendary innovators as Victor Vasnetsov and Alexandre Benois, one of the founders of *World of Art* and a fierce opponent of the academic painters who were also represented in the list. We also learn that the cards had a charitable purpose, the beneficiaries being a house of nursing nuns, the Community of St. Eugenia of the Red Cross, who had founded a publishing office of their own that played a major role in the development of Russian pre-revolutionary postcards. Over twenty years, the Community's press published over six thousand designs. Nearly every surviving Russian family archive contains one or more cards emblazoned with the sign of the Red Cross.

In 1926, on the thirtieth anniversary of this publishing house, Benois (who was by then living in France) wrote to Ivan Stepanov, its founder and head, expressing his admiration for him and for the 'gigantic card-index' he had assembled: 'In this relatively modest field, you have created something truly great, something wonderful. No one has made a finer contribution to our Russian mass education.'[5]

Apraksin Dvor, a covered market in St. Petersburg, situated between Sadovaya Street and the Fontanka River. Built in the mid-nineteenth century on a much older trading site, it was a centre for all sorts of goods – furs, furniture, shoes, spices, groceries and wine.

Of all the graphic design of the period covered by this book, only the works of the World of Art group – along with those of the Russian Futurists – are widely known and enjoy a secure place in the history of art. All the rest have remained in obscurity until now, for three main reasons. First, after the Bolshevik revolution of 1917 the new government and its new art establishment were determined to obliterate everything connected with pre-revolutionary Russia; second, the world-wide interest in the Russian avant-garde of the 1910s and 1920s has overshadowed the achievements of 'pre-avant-garde' art; and finally, it is a general rule that whatever already enjoys recognition more easily attracts the attention of the public at large. Much of the material published here has been languishing deep in the archives of the Rumyantsev Museum public library (now the Lenin Library) for nearly one hundred years, in the very heart of Moscow and in full view of the Kremlin.

СВЩ: ВҢ ИХ ПРЕО СУРЪ ИМПРТРЪ АЛЕКСАНДРА III И ГСДРН ИМПРАТРИЦЫ МАРІИ ѲЕОДОРОВНЫ

Борщекъ и похлебка.
Пирожки.
Стерляди паровыя.
Телятина.
Заливное.
Жаркое цыплята и дичь.
Спаржа.
Гурьевская каша.
Мороженое.

1883 года Мая

2

1

THE STYLE RUSSE

Let us begin with what may seem a rather provocative statement. All the Russian art of the second half of the nineteenth century (taken as a whole, and including the field of graphic design with which we are here concerned) springs from Russian literature, which attained truly great stature during this period, and whose development was accompanied by inspired literary criticism. The century fully deserves its reputation as the golden age of Russian literature.

It was literary criticism that shaped the views of the non-aristocratic intelligentsia, the most influential social group in the country from the mid 1850s onwards. The critics of the time did not restrict themselves exclusively to literary matters; they were also driven by the desire to participate in social and political life, and to encourage progressive thinking about how society might be transformed. The most prominent figures – such as Vissarion Belinsky, Dimitrii Pisarev, Nikolai Chernyshevsky and Nikolai Dobrolyubov – were born ideologues as well as fierce and lucid publicists. They personified the Russian revolutionary and democratic movement. For them, literature was not an end in itself but the only means, given the existence of absolute monarchy and strict censorship, for them to propagate their ideas and express their revolutionary aspirations.

The literary and aesthetic opinions of these commentators were determined by their civic and political interests. They were convinced that art must now be of some practical use, meet human needs and subordinate itself to the demands of real life. The 'usefulness' of art resided in its content, which ought always to promote social and moral progress. This utilitarian approach demanded that art should become the means of achieving the most urgent social and political reforms; the satisfaction of aesthetic requirements was only secondary. Chernyshevsky's theory of aesthetics exerted a powerful and lasting influence on the minds of Russian artists. He established a strict hierarchical system according to which life was placed higher than art, literature above the other arts, and content above form.

Henceforward, Russians were to acknowledge the unquestionable primacy and authority of literature and to regard men of letters as prophets and advocates, indeed as the guardians of the nation's moral and social conscience. This determined the fate of the visual arts in general, which, together with aesthetic and artistic education, were relegated to a position of secondary importance in the public mind.

1
Victor Vasnetsov, St. Petersburg, 1883
Menu for a luncheon in honour of the
Coronation of Their Imperial Majesties
Alexander III and Maria Fedorovna,
detail (see no. 9).

2
Ivan Bilibin, St. Petersburg, 1900
Illumination for 'Vasilisa the
Magnificent', a Russian folk-tale.
6 × 8¾ in. (15 × 22.5 cm.)

Ivan Bilibin
Born near St. Petersburg, 1876; died in
Leningrad, 1942. Graduated from the
Law Faculty of St. Petersburg University.
Attended lectures at the St. Petersburg
Academy of Arts; studied with Repin.
Joined the World of Art group in 1900.
Bilibin was the first Russian artist to
dedicate himself to the profession of
graphic design. He developed a graphic
style of his own with its roots in Russian
popular art. His skilful use of old Russian
typefaces, his ethnographic accuracy,
firmness of line, a strong decorative
talent and the rich imagination of a born
story-teller make up the 'Bilibin style' and
characterize all his work, which includes
book and magazine design, posters,
postcards, publishers' marks and logos,
and theatre programmes. Bilibin was the
most accomplished exponent of the
Neo-Russian Style in graphic art.

3
Ivan Bilibin, St. Petersburg, 1905
Illustration for 'The Tale of Tsar Saltan', a
story by Alexander Pushkin.
8½ × 10¾ in. (21.5 × 27.5 cm.)

4
Ivan Bilibin, St. Petersburg, 1905
Illustration for 'The Tale of Tsar Saltan'.
5 × 10¾ in. (13 × 27.5 cm.)

Literary criticism, as the principal expression of the social and aesthetic mood of the era, strongly affected progressively minded commentators on art and architecture, who similarly concerned themselves with the social, civic and didactic usefulness of the arts. The revolutionary and democratic ideals of the 1840s, 1850s and 1860s nourished the generation of artists active after 1870.

The central figure and leading critic of the time was Vasily Stasov, whose field was, in fact, art rather than literature. He was a man of immense stature and authority, whose opinions dominated artistic life and influenced the work of painters and architects – and also of composers – for some fifty years.

What kind of art developed during this period, and how was it influenced by literature and literary criticism? The work of the so-called Wanderers *(peredvizhniki,* or members of the Society for Travelling Art Exhibitions, which organized shows all over the Empire), many of them well-known artists such as Ilya Repin, Vladimir Makovsky and Ivan Kramskoi, earned plaudits from the public and the whole-hearted support of Stasov. They concentrated largely on genre subjects, borrowing fresh and untried themes from everyday life which reflected the simple concerns of simple folk. Taking their lead from literature, the Wanderers enthusiastically added their own lively social critique to their convincing recreations of reality.

The demand for a non-elitist and popular culture led to a single-minded critical concentration on the ideas and content of works of art. A new and socially relevant theme was often sufficient in itself to earn the artist the highest praise in reviews, which might well contain a detailed analysis of the subject of a work without a single word about its expressive and artistic merits. (Incidentally, this approach has retained its power until very recently. Recent research shows that, replying to questions about Russian painters known to the respondents, most people still mention the subjects of specific paintings rather than the artists who created them.)

This primacy of theme and content above form was equally evident in the field of graphic design. Russian (and, later, Soviet) graphics have always displayed a strong tendency towards realistic drawing and real situations, as is well illustrated in the present book. The painter Yelizaveta Bem, for example, enjoyed an unprecedented popularity in the early years of the present century for her series of postcards depicting sentimental scenes of the lives of peasant children. And yet a review in *Art and Industrial Design,* which had organized a postcard competition, commented that '. . . most of her cards are simply little pictures, miniature vignettes and drawings which seem to have landed on the card by sheer chance; nothing in their composition indicates that they were actually designed for cards at all'.[6] Similarly, Sergei Diaghilev wrote in the *World of Art* journal, reviewing the profusely illustrated centenary edition of Pushkin's works: '. . . this is an album which includes drawings by all the most

3

4

talented Russian painters of our day . . . but the three volumes contain hardly a single true "illustration" .'[7]

Incomparably greater attention is paid to content than to form in Russian graphic design. This bias gives it its distinctive character and also explains the reluctance of many of its practitioners to experiment with new techniques. Those artists who did not subscribe to the prevalent aesthetic norms and principles of the nineteenth century were always in a minority in Russia, and any deviation from accepted views on the relationship between form and content was seen as a sign of Western influence.

The most hotly debated issue of the day was the question of how Russia was to develop after the emancipation of the peasants: should she choose the Western, capitalist model, or find a solution of her own? Perhaps nowhere in nineteenth-century Europe was the need to solve problems of national identity and self-definition as urgent as it was in Russia. As a result, most attention was concentrated on the problem of national self-determination, the search for national roots and the reinterpretation of the past. Discussion centred around the relationship between Russia and the West and fanned the controversy between the 'Slavophiles' and the 'Westerners'.

In this context of nationalist fervour, the creation of a new style in architecture – the most influential of the arts of design – was seen as nothing less than a patriotic duty and a social obligation. The style appropriate to the new Russia must, of course, be both new and Russian. This truism, however, contained a paradox: the new style – intended to serve generations yet to come – was entirely based on themes and motifs derived from the heritage of Russian culture. What became known as the *style russe* or Russian Style was, in essence, just one manifestation of the general trend.

From the 1840s and '50s until almost the end of the nineteenth century and the spread of Art Nouveau, architectural development was restricted to borrowing from the forms of the historic – rather than the imaginary – past. It would have been inconceivable for architects to work outside the 'styles' derived in this way. During the whole of the century, the only changes in architectural thinking had to do with the principles on which the choice of historical models was based. The sources of inspiration were constantly widened to include new forms of national culture, but the historical approach itself remained unchanged, as did the conviction that the new style could only be shaped by the themes and motifs of the past.

The result was eclecticism. Innovation was tied to the ability freely to combine forms derived from various historical sources and to improvise simultaneously, so to speak, on various themes (for reliance on any one particular style was considered slavishly imitative). A high value was attached to the architect's ability to make use of unusual details borrowed from the past while combining them in

5

fresh and untraditional compositions. Nineteenth-century architecture appealed to a well-developed sense of history and a familiarity with a range of different styles. Today we often find it difficult to distinguish between the views and work of architects who, to their contemporaries, epitomized quite different periods in the Russian style (and who were continually at odds with each other).

The Russian Style, then, was based exclusively on Russian historical material. It did not tell the artist which artistic sources (for example, which type of architecture) to use, or which periods in history should be considered as most essentially 'Russian', that is, most fully representative of the spiritual uniqueness of the Russian people. It was typical of the times that attempts were made to solve this problem on a strictly scientific basis. Among professionals the conviction grew stronger that a new architecture could be achieved only by the application of scientific analysis to historical forms.

Historians called for the serious study of the monuments of the past and for a comprehensive, systematic collection of historical material. Monuments were accurately measured, and the carved wooden decorations from peasant log houses were meticulously collected. A succession of fundamental works on Russian ornamental design were published. Viktor Gartman, one of the best-known architects working within the Russian style, published an album of folk embroidery to which Stasov contributed a foreword. Equally characteristic of this period was a book by Butovsky entitled *A History of Russian Ornamental Design from the Tenth to the Sixteenth Centuries. Based on Ancient*

5
Ivan Bilibin, St. Petersburg, 1905
Illustration for 'The Tale of Tsar Saltan'.
14½ × 16½ in. (36 × 41.5 cm.)

6
Ivan Bilibin, St. Petersburg, 1900
Illumination for 'Maria Morevna', a
Russian folk-tale.
3 × 8 in. (7.5 × 20 cm.)

Manuscripts, which was illustrated by accurately reproduced examples, enlarged details and elaborate schematic diagrams. As the author put it: 'This book is aimed exclusively at the needs of technical and industrial designers. It is intended to introduce Russian craftsmen to the models and sources for an original Russian style.'[8]

Stasov, who set the tone for all thinking about art, was a tireless advocate of everything truly Russian and 'folk' in the new art and made a great practical contribution to the development of the Russian Style. The year 1887 saw the publication of his definitive study, in three volumes, of *Slav and Eastern Ornamental Design in Ancient and Modern Manuscripts,* in which he gave a systematic account of material he had been collecting for more than twenty-five years. In the compilation of his survey, Stasov had searched through literally all the great public and private libraries of Russia and Europe, travelling to London and Paris alone on no less than six separate occasions. The aim of the work was frankly practical: 'My survey is capable of a highly practical application in several fields of industrial design, through the introduction of many previously unknown examples of various Slavic and Eastern styles of ancient and modern times.'[9]

The drawings in Stasov's book were by Ivan Ropet, his favourite architect. Such was the fervour with which Stasov supported his work that Ropet's style became synonymous with the Russian Style itself. Curiously, the pseudonym Ropet sounds distinctly foreign, whereas his real name – Ivan Petrov – could hardly have been more Russian.

What was it about Ropet's architectural style that so attracted Stasov? The critic considered the emergence of a new content in architecture to be of overriding importance; he believed this content must include elements of national character, and that it could only be achieved through the use of themes derived from folk architecture. (Here again we encounter the familiar pattern of thought, summed up in the phrase 'from content to form', that dominated the aesthetic approach of the revolutionary democrats.) Ropet's work, which abundantly exploited motifs borrowed from peasant and other wooden architecture, fully satisfied these requirements.

Ropet practised only one of many versions of the Russian Style; but his importance goes beyond architecture itself. He was directly involved in the formation of the Russian Style in graphic design. Books lavishly designed by him became models of their kind, and his personal graphic language had a tremendous impact on the graphic design of the period.

The Russian Style was not only highly recognizable in itself but further distinguished by the richness with which its vast quantity of detail was applied. Stasov and his contemporaries were entranced by lavishly decorated objects. Even the small selection of graphic works illustrated in these pages provides a vivid impression of the abundance and variety of decor, which in our eyes verges on excess, but which was then considered the height of artistic achievement.

No account of the Russian Style would be complete without the inclusion of the painter Victor Vasnetsov. He occupied a central position in the cultural life of the 1890s, when the novelty of the Wanderers was losing its lustre and their themes were already exhausted. He was a man of universal gifts, who created the murals for the Historical Museum in Moscow and the Cathedral of St. Vladimir in Kiev and designed the façade of the Tretyakov Gallery. He enriched the national heritage with many paintings, book illustrations, posters and much more besides. His work was loved by all sections of society. His major paintings introduced new themes borrowed from Russian folklore, fairy-tale and legend; and his contemporaries welcomed his every new work with undiminished delight and admiration.

6

In a way, Vasnetsov's work has itself become part of the national folklore. His Bogatyri (heroes of Russian folklore and defenders of the Motherland) and his Alyonushka (the protagonist of a well-known fairy-tale) are still the favourite themes of mass-produced kitsch. The secret of the enduring popularity of his images is that they are easily understood and richly allusive illustrations of popular literature.

It was Vasnetsov who first introduced themes from folklore into graphic design. They were particularly popular at the beginning of the twentieth century among the artists of what became known as the Neo-Russian Style.

Rooted though it is in folklore, Neo-Russian design is unmistakably a product of the same international search for new, non-historicist forms that produced Art Nouveau (the subject of the following chapter). Vasnetsov's versatility is itself a very Art Nouveau phenomenon, as is the stylization that in this context is both 'new' and 'Russian'.

Themes from peasant and folk art appear in the Neo-Russian Style, but – by contrast with the Russian Style proper – always in a stylized manner, The traditional motifs, however, remain recognizable, and this gives Neo-Russian its characteristically archaic air. From our perspective, at any rate, works in the Neo-Russian Style seem closer to those of the pure Russian Style than to those of Art Nouveau. The thematic affinities tend to outweigh the differences of artistic idiom.

In all the international exhibitions of the early years of this century, beginning with the 1900 World Exposition in Paris, Russia was represented by Neo-Russian art. The architecture of the pavilions, as well as examples of craft work and graphics, delighted the public with exotic designs whose unfamiliar, organic forms were strikingly different from those of the Western European exhibits.

The conceptual basis of Neo-Russian form was developed by Moscow artists whose work straddled the separate artistic 'colonies' created by two late nineteenth-century patrons of the arts: Abramtsevo, the estate near Moscow owned by Savva Mamontov, and Talashkino, Princess Maria Tenisheva's estate near Smolensk. All the great artists of the time gathered at one or other of these centres, and many young artists made their debuts there. The generosity of their hosts enabled them to spend long periods in the country, working and resting.

At Abramtsevo in the 1880s and 1890s, the resident artists lived as one family, going for leisurely walks, drawing, drinking tea and staging amateur theatricals. In the free and easy atmosphere of the colony, they endlessly debated such questions as the duty of the artistic intelligentsia, how art could serve the people, the relationship between beauty and utility, the rejection of the existing social order and the need to transform life by means of art. But the underlying concern of all these conversations was with the national art of Russia: what it should be, where to seek its roots, the nature of the national ideal, and how to achieve the organic quality so evident in folk art.

Abramtsevo was the scene of the formal quest that was to produce the Neo-Russian Style; Talashkino saw its heyday and consummation. The artists who went to Talashkino to work and to organize its craft workshops were deliberately dedicating their creative energies to the renewal of the traditions of folk art. They devised a language for the new style, explored its potential, and finally produced what we now recognize as the classic examples of Neo-Russian design.

7
Ivan Bilibin, St. Petersburg, 1905
Illustration for 'The Tale of the
Fisherman and the Fish', a story by
Alexander Pushkin.

8
Unknown artist, St. Petersburg, no date.
Wrapper for Boyarsky Chocolate, one
of a series.
3½ × 2¾ in. (8.5 × 7 cm.)

9
Victor Vasnetsov, St. Petersburg, 1883
Menu for a dinner in honour of the
Coronation of Their Imperial Majesties
Alexander III and Maria Fedorovna.
Menu: clear beetroot soup and broth,
pies, steamed sterlets (fish), veal, aspic,
roasts, chicken and game, asparagus,
gurevskaya kasha (a dish of semolina,
dried and fresh fruit, nuts and honey)
and ice-cream.
31½ × 10¾ in. (79 × 27 cm.)

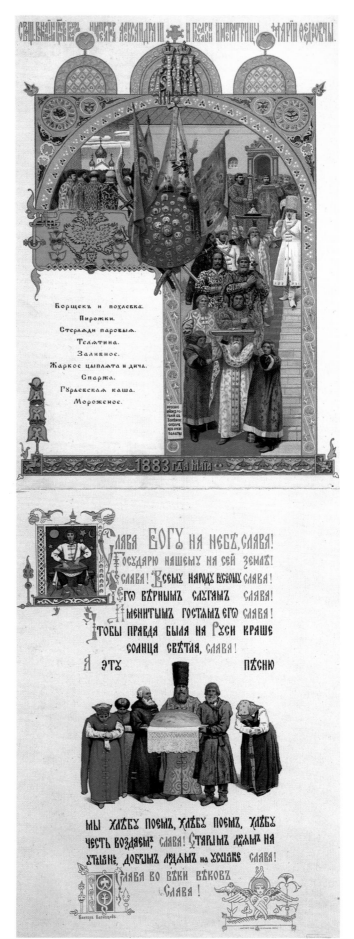

10
Victor Vasnetsov, St. Petersburg, 1883
Dinner menu for 27 May 1883; cream of
mushroom soup, bouillon with herbs,
pies, sterlets with cucumber, boiled beef,
quail with ground peas, cold crayfish,
roast turkey with snipe, salad, asparagus
with Hollandaise sauce, hot pineapple
pie, ice-cream and dessert.
16½ × 10 in. (41 × 25 cm.)

11
Unknown artist, St. Petersburg, no date
Wrapper for Boyarsky Chocolate, one
of a series.
3½ × 2¾ in. (8.5 × 7 cm.)

12
N. Krasnov, Moscow, 1887
Menu for a breakfast on New Year's Day
1887, to celebrate the hundredth
anniversary of Vassily Perlov & Sons:
mixed hors-d'oeuvres, oysters, bouillon,
royal galantine, suckling-pig in cream
(from Perlov & Sons), various kulebyaki
(fish or meat in pastry), paté of game
with truffles, trout Gachina, Siberian
white salmon, Visland salmon,
Kuchugursk sturgeon, roast beef, ham,
veal, salt beef, cucumbers *Nezhin*,
turkey, capons, Caucasian pheasant,
Siberian hazel-grouse, mixed salads.
For dessert were almonds, nuts,
pears and apples.
18½ × 12¾ in. (46 × 32 cm.)

ОБѢДЪ

27 МАЯ.

СУПЪ ПЮРЕ ИЗЪ ГРИБОВЪ

БУЛЬОНЪ СЪ КОРЕНЬЯМИ

ПИРОЖКИ

СТЕРЛЯДИ СЪ ОГУРЦАМИ

ГОВЯДИНА РАЗВАРНАЯ

ПЕРЕПЕЛА СЪ ТЕРТЫМЪ ГОРОХОМЪ

ХОЛОДНОЕ ИЗЪ РАКОВЪ

ЖАРКОЕ ИНДѢЙКА И БЕКАСЫ

САЛАДЪ

СПАРЖА СОУСЪ ГОЛЛАНДСКІЙ

ПИРОГЪ ГОРЯЧІЙ СЪ АНАНАСАМИ

МОРОЖЕНОЕ

ДЕССЕРТЪ

13

14

15

13

I. Nevinsky, Moscow, 1900
Menu for Easter dinner of 11 April 1900, originally rolled in a brocade cover. The menu included *paskha* (a sweet cream-cheese dish eaten at Easter), *kulichi* (Easter cake), eggs, chicken soup, swan, peacock, pheasant, turkey, hazel-grouse, partridge, quail, spring lamb, ham, suckling-pig with horseradish, beef on the bone, roast chicken, cold red partridge, chopped liver and sea crayfish.
21½ × 8½ in. (54 × 21.5 cm.)

14

Victor Vasnetsov, St. Petersburg, 1906
Menu for a breakfast on 26 November 1906, to commemorate the anniversary of the establishment of Russia's highest military order, the Cross of St. George. The menu consisted of: soups 'Peter the Great' and 'Princess', with pies, Dvina sterlet in champagne, saddle of lamb, French poulard with truffles, ice-cream and dessert.
15 × 13¾ in. (37.5 × 34.5 cm.)

15

Unknown artist, St. Petersburg, no date
Wrapper for Boyarsky Chocolate, one of a series.
3½ × 2¾ in. (8.5 × 7 cm.)

16

S. Yaguzhinsky, Moscow, 1913
Menu for a dinner on 25 May 1913, given in honour of the three-hundredth anniversary of the founding of the Romanov dynasty: turtle soup and cream of chicken and asparagus, pies, sterlet Imperial, saddle of wild goat *garni*, chicken with truffles, punch 'Viktoria', roasts: duck and poulard, cucumber salad, asparagus with sauce, peaches 'Cardinal', Parisian ice-cream and dessert.
17½ × 6½ in. (44 × 16 cm.)

16

17

18

19

17
Victor Vasnetsov, Moscow, 1896
Supper menu of 20 May 1896 on the
occasion of the Coronation of Nicholas II
and Alexandra Fedorovna: partridge soup
with various pies, sterlet à l'Italienne,
roast poulard and game, Swiss salad, and
ice-cream with raspberry sauce.
17½ × 12½ in. (44 × 31 cm.)

18
Victor Vasnetsov, Moscow, 1896
Menu for a dinner on 14 May 1896 on
the occasion of the Coronation of Their
Imperial Majesties Nicholas II and
Alexandra Fedorovna: *Rassolnik* soup
(meat or fish soup with pickled
cucumbers), clear beetroot soup with
pies, steamed sterlet, roast lamb, capons,
salad, asparagus, and pheasant in aspic.
For dessert there were fruits in wine and
ice-cream.
38 × 13¼ in. (95 × 33 cm.)

19
Unknown artist, St. Petersburg, no date
Wrapper for Boyarsky Chocolate, one
of a series.
3½ × 2¾ in. (8.5 × 7 cm.)

20
B. Zvorykin, Moscow, 1910
Menu for a banquet on 22 February 1910
in honour of a delegation from the
French parliament.
13½ × 10 in. (34 × 25 cm.)

21
B. Zvorykin, Moscow, 1912
Programme for a reception arranged at
the City Duma (Town Hall).
14½ × 8½ in. (36 × 21 cm.)

22
Alexandre Benois, Moscow, 1896
Dinner menu for 15 May 1896 on the
occasion of the Coronation of Nicholas II
and Alexandra Fedorovna.
14¾ × 10¾ in. (37 × 27 cm.)

20

21

22

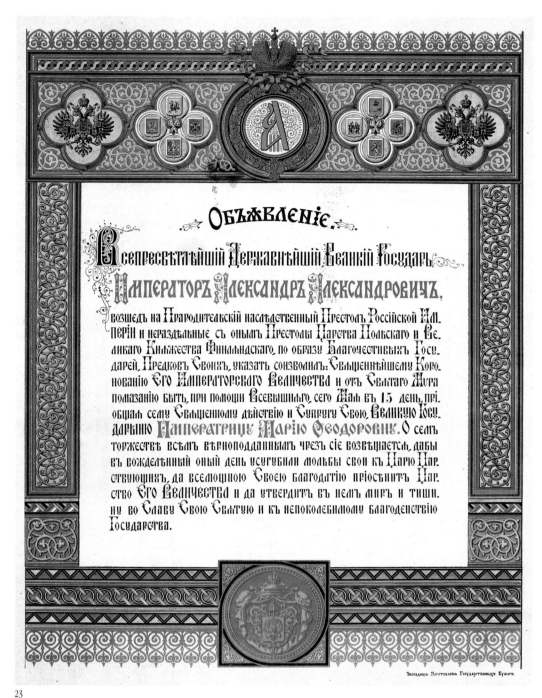

23

25

23
Unknown artist, Moscow, 1881
Announcement of the Emperor Alexander III's ukase on the Coronation of the Empress Maria Fedorovna.
13½ × 10½ in. (33.5 × 26 cm.)

24
Unknown artist, Moscow, no date
Design from a form for the Mayor of the City of Moscow. Centre: Moscow coat of arms – St. George Pobedonosets (bearer of victory).
3½ × 7½ in. (9 × 19 cm.)

25
Unknown artist, no date

26
Example of typeface in 'Russian style' from the Leman type-foundry.

27
Ivan Ropet, Moscow, 1896
Announcement of the Coronation of the Emperor Nicholas II and the Empress Alexandra Fedorovna on 14 May 1896.
16½ × 11½ in. (41 × 28.5 cm.)

26

24

28

28
Imperial double-headed eagle with crown
and the date, '1613', the beginning of the
Romanov dynasty.

29
B. Zvorykin, Moscow, 1912
Theatre programme cover for the
Imperial Bolshoi Theatre.
13½ × 9½ in. (34 × 24 cm.)

30
B. Zvorykin, Moscow, 1914
Concert programme cover for 10 January
1914 to celebrate the anniversary of fifty
years' publication of 'Regulations for
Gubernatorial and Regional Zemstvos'
(the elected district councils) from
1864 to 1917.
The text reads: 'Father Tsar, the Russian
Zemstvo bows down before thee!'
11¾ × 8 in. (29.5 × 20 cm.)

31
B. Zvorykin, Moscow, 1913
Theatre programme cover for the
Imperial Alexander Theatre. In 1913 the
three-hundredth anniversary of the
Romanov dynasty was widely celebrated
in Russia.
14¼ × 8¾ in. (35.5 × 22 cm.)

32
S. Yaguzhinsky, Moscow, 1913
Front and back of a menu cover for a
luncheon 'in celebration of the 300th
anniversary of the House of Romanov'.
Left, the Autocrat Mikhail Fedorovich,
founder of the dynasty, right, Nicholas II,
last Emperor of Russia.
9¼ × 13½ in. (23 × 33.5 cm.)

29

30

31

32

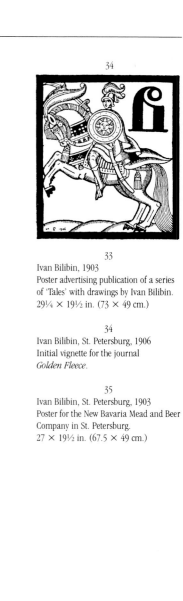

33

Ivan Bilibin, 1903
Poster advertising publication of a series
of 'Tales' with drawings by Ivan Bilibin.
29¼ × 19½ in. (73 × 49 cm.)

34

Ivan Bilibin, St. Petersburg, 1906
Initial vignette for the journal
Golden Fleece.

35

Ivan Bilibin, St. Petersburg, 1903
Poster for the New Bavaria Mead and Beer
Company in St. Petersburg.
27 × 19½ in. (67.5 × 49 cm.)

36

37

38

36
Unknown artist, St. Petersburg, 1909
Poster for an international exhibition of
the latest discoveries of the all-Russian
aeroclub.
42½ × 29¼ in. (106 × 73 cm.)

37
A. Burnovo, St. Petersburg, 1909
Poster for an 'International Exhibition of
Beer-brewing, Production of Hops and
other plants, and Machine Construction'.
43¼ × 25½ in. (108 × 64 cm.)

38
Ivan Bilibin, St. Petersburg, 1906
Initial vignette for the journal
Golden Fleece.

39
Ye. Firsov, St. Petersburg, 1909
Poster for an international exhibition
(Kazan, 1909) of light industry,
professional training and agriculture,
with sections devoted to heavy industry
and fire-fighting.
21½ × 14¾ in. (54 × 37 cm.)

42

40
A. Paramonov, St. Petersburg, 1901
Poster for an exhibition of folk crafts,
sponsored by the Society for the
Encouragement of Handicrafts.
44 × 26 in. (110 × 65 cm.)

41
A. Burnovo, St. Petersburg, 1908
Poster for the 'International Exhibition
of Industrial Design in Furniture,
Decorative Work, Furnishings
and Fittings'.
34¾ × 22¾ in. (87 × 57 cm.)

42
Ivan Bilibin, St. Petersburg, 1906
Initial vignette for the journal
Golden Fleece.

43
Mikhail Vrubel, Moscow, 1901
Poster for the 'Exhibition of 36 Artists',
including the names of all thirty-six
participants.
24½ × 18¾ in. (61 × 47 cm.)

43

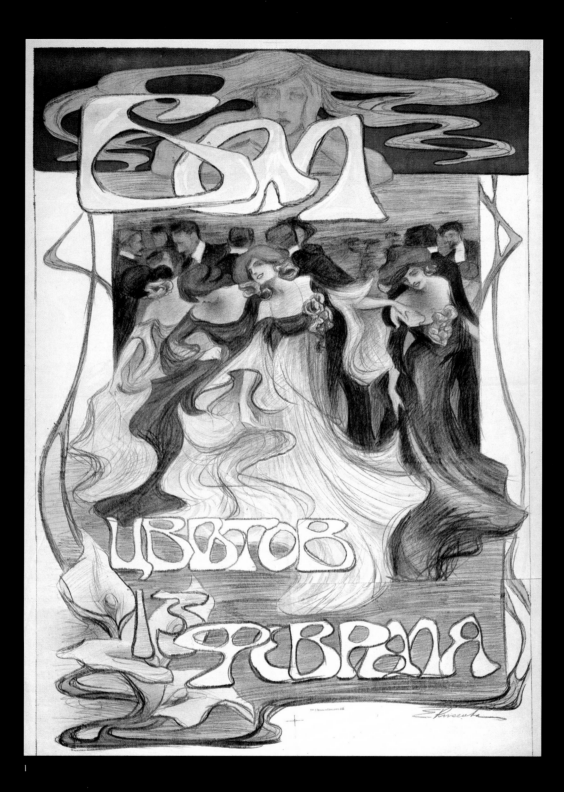

2

THE *MODERNE*: RUSSIAN ART NOUVEAU

By contrast with the Russian and Neo-Russian styles, it is tempting to describe the style discussed in this chapter as 'Western'. Contemporaries, no doubt, found the differences even more acute, especially because the new style burst upon an artistic milieu still utterly dominated by nineteenth-century tastes. In Russian – as in English – the Art Nouveau style was given a name derived from French; in printed Russian texts, indeed, the word *moderne* was usually given in French, and in the Roman alphabet. It may well be that the term came into general use in Russia after the 1900 World Exposition in Paris, though no research has yet been done to decide the question one way or the other.

This should not be taken to imply that *moderne* took hold in Russia only after 1900, or that Russian culture 'imported' it from Europe. The drastic transformation of artistic thinking which resulted in the new style was determined by changes in the fabric of society and occurred almost simultaneously in the cultures of a number of countries besides Russia. Russia found its own route to Art Nouveau, which then manifested itself in a distinctive way. From the mid-1890s (at the latest) onwards, all artistic life was in the thrall of the new approach; it was indubitably an idea whose time had come. The 'new style' had acquired theoretical as well as practical reality.

All the same, the themes and motifs most characteristic of the new style – those that distinguished it from all other styles – were indeed borrowed by Russia from Western Europe. The present chapter is devoted to *moderne* as a Russian version of 'cosmopolitan' Art Nouveau. Although *moderne* had some indigenous features, essentially the style was a foreign one.

It was inevitable that the long evolution of nineteenth-century culture would sooner or later give way to the creation of a new artistic style, no mere passing fashion but a total renewal of artistic taste, ideals, values and forms. 'Art Nouveau', 'Jugendstil', 'Liberty', and 'Secession' were among the terms used to describe the new style in various countries. It was the beginning of an era when national cultures were becoming increasingly international in character. The World Exposition which marked the turn of the century was the forum for *le style moderne,* and Paris promoted it to the height of fashion.

The new style was everywhere seen as progressive and democratic, addressed at once to the whole of society and to each individual member of it. The ambition of its practitioners was to introduce art into the everyday world and, in the process, to transform social life itself.

1
E. Kiseleva, St. Petersburg, 1903
Poster for the 13 February
'Ball of Flowers'.
36¾ × 27¼ in. (92 × 68 cm.)

2
Unknown artist, St. Petersburg, 1901
Detail of poster (see no. 12).

In June 1897, Konstantin Stanislavsky met Vladimir Nemirovich-Danchenko in the elegant surroundings of the Slavyansky Bazaar restaurant in Moscow. Their conversation was to have important consequences for the history of Russian culture. For about eighteen hours, they discussed the creation of a new Russian theatre. 'No world conference could have debated vital questions of state more thoroughly than we discussed the principles of our new enterprise, questions of pure art, our artistic ideals, theatre ethics, technique and even organizational problems', as Stanislavsky later recalled.[10]

They named their creation the Moscow Art Theatre for All; the words 'art' and 'for all' vividly and deliberately expressed their artistic credo. The joint ambition of these two great theatrical innovators was to stage plays that would satisfy the highest artistic standards and be aimed at the widest possible public, an aspiration which truly reflected the aesthetic and ethical ideals of the time.

Equally typical of this spirit was the decision of the millionaire industrialist and patron of the arts, Sergei Morozov, to finance the building of the theatre, which was designed without fee by the most prominent architect of the *moderne,* Fyodor Shekhtel.

3
M. Belsky (?), Moscow, 1900s
Soap wrapper, prototype.
6¾ × 7½ in. (17 × 19 cm.)

4
M. Belsky (?), Moscow, 1900s
Soap wrapper, prototype.
6¾ × 7¼ in. (17 × 18 cm.)

3

4

The principal idea behind the new artistic thinking was that of a 'synthesis of the arts', including the concept of the necessity for a total, all-embracing treatment of any object – whether an architectural structure, an interior, a book or anything else. This fostered the interaction of the various arts and the development of universally gifted individuals. The versatility of such artists as William Morris and Henry van der Velde – and in Russia that of Victor Vasnetsov, Mikhail Vrubel and Fyodor Shekhtel – was typical of this new breed.

'The theatre begins at the cloakroom': Stanislavsky's epigrammatic phrase tells us much about the artistic outlook of the leading figures of Russian Art Nouveau. We know that Shekhtel, one of its most talented representatives, carefully calculated every detail of his designs, from the functional arrangement of space (the stage, dressing-rooms and other working spaces planned for ease and convenience of use) to the forms of such objects as the furniture, lights and signs. He put Stanislavsky's ideals into practice by creating an environment that matched to perfection the atmosphere evoked on stage. The unique aesthetic personality of the Moscow Art Theatre was formed in this single-minded insistence on the organic synthesis of all the constituent parts of the enterprise. A

5
M. Belsky (?), Moscow, 1900s
Soap wrapper, prototype.
6½ × 7½ in. (16.5 × 19 cm.)

6
M. Belsky (?), Moscow, 1900s
Soap wrapper, prototype.
7 × 7¼ in. (17.5 × 18 cm.)

5

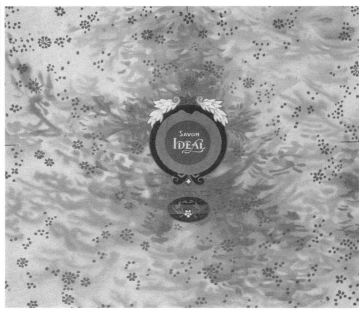

6

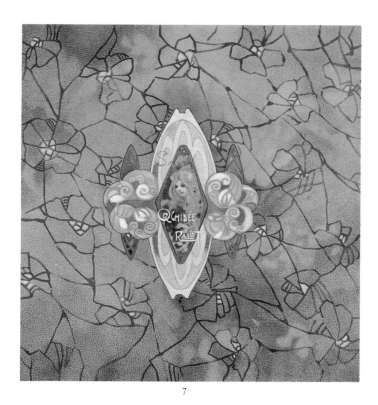

7

8

truly Russian theatre, born from within Russian culture, the Moscow Art Theatre also expressed the aesthetic aspirations common to all of Art Nouveau.

The new style was intended to bring about entirely new forms and to obliterate the old historical approach. In their search for the new, artists turned to nature for inspiration. Nature was the principal source of those distinctive organic forms that identified the new style – the sinuous, twisting lines found in roots and plant stems were the ideal models.

It is, of course, impossible fully to comprehend the process by which the aspirations of individual artists gradually cohere into a unified movement. In the *moderne*, we may observe an unusually clear agreement of tastes and views among the very different artists who seemed to have struck quite independently on the same subjects and moods.

Art Nouveau is a feminine style – as Constructivism was to be masculine. Its ideals were beauty, poetry and nature. It prized most highly such qualities as refinement, delicacy and spirituality. Its preferred forms were lithe, flowing, shimmering and pliant, its colours subtle and unfamiliar. Thus, it is rich in those elegant flowers – irises, lilies, chrysanthemums, orchids – that adorned the wallpapers and book-covers of London and St. Petersburg. Another common passion was for waves, the sea and the underwater kingdom. And, of course, the image of woman is integral to Art Nouveau. In graphic art, its quintessential image was created by Alphonse Mucha, whose muse was the actress Sarah Bernhardt.

Shekhtel's favourite theme, which he interpreted in many different ways and always included in his designs, was that of the wave. It is to be found in the nobly restrained interior of the Art Theatre. The pattern running along the top of the smooth walls of the foyer, the decoration on the metal plates on the upper parts of the doors, the frieze in the auditorium and the strip of appliqué on the drop curtain – the total design – is based on a stylized geometry of wavelike forms, while at the centre of the curtain, where the audience's attention is most intently focused, we see a white gull in flight against a background of waves.

Waves and a gull: here we have the very essence of Russian Art Nouveau. However, the gull on the Moscow Art Theatre curtain is more than just a symbol of flight, more even than a tribute to the style itself. It is Chekhov's Seagull. The Moscow Art Theatre staged several of Chekhov's plays, of which *The Seagull* was the first. It was here, in fact, that Chekhov was first introduced to the world at large: after the failure of its premiere in St. Petersburg, the play's success in Moscow ensured a great future for the author as well as for the Art Theatre itself, and he wrote all his later plays specifically with Stanislavsky's brainchild in mind.

Chekhov was a contemporary of *moderne,* and his plays are a true reflection of life; to read them is to learn how Russians lived. 'It's new forms we need, new forms!' exclaims a character in *The Seagull.* Shekhtel's seagull became the emblem of the Moscow Art Theatre for All.

The demand for new forms manifested itself in the search for new themes and sources of inspiration, but it also had a profound effect on the way artists actually expressed themselves. To put it

7
M. Belsky (?), Moscow, 1900s
Soap wrapper, prototype.
8½ × 8 in. (21 × 20 cm.)

8
M. Belsky (?) Moscow, 1900s
Soap wrapper, prototype.
6¾ × 7½ in. (17 × 19 cm.)

9
M. Belsky (?) Moscow, 1900s
Soap wrapper, prototype.
6¾ × 7½ in. (17 × 19 cm.)

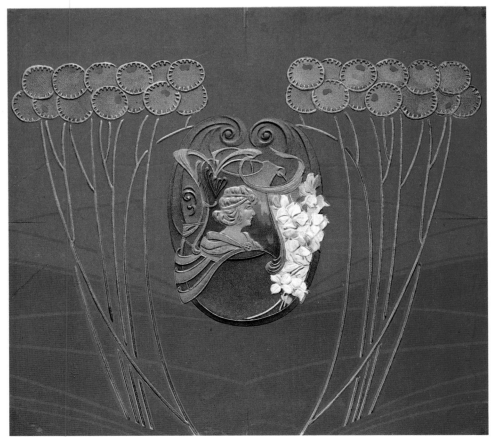

9

another way, the new style brought about changes in the manner as well as in the object of depiction; the dominant principle of *moderne* is stylization.

In Art Nouveau, creative stylization replaced the merely imitative manner associated with eclecticism. The imitative artist, whatever the form on which he based his design, was attempting to preserve its every detail and all the accuracy of its original proportions: that is, literally to copy it. The stylizing artist, on the other hand, approached his form in a very different way, his intention being to convey an overall image and to emphasize certain individual features while diminishing others. He was quite prepared to sacrifice detail for the sake of the whole: in other words, to subordinate form to his creative will, to distance form from its prototype. We may characterize the imitator as passive, trustful and naïve; the stylizer is active, self-confident and ambitious.

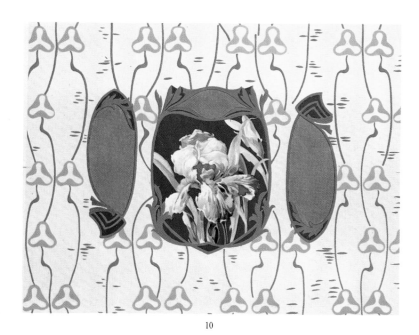

10

11

10
M. Belsky (?) Moscow, 1900s
Soap wrapper, prototype.
7¼ × 7¾ in. (18 × 19.5 cm.)

11
Unknown artist, St. Petersburg, 1901
Poster for a technical students'
Concert Ball.
30¾ × 22½ in. (77 × 56 cm.)

12
Unknown artist, St. Petersburg, 1901
Poster for the Passage Concert Hall.
30¾ × 22¾ in. (77 × 57 cm.)

12

14

13
N. Vysheslavtsev, Moscow, 1900s
Poster for the film *Tais.*
46¾ × 32 in. (117 × 80 cm.)

14
N. Kalmakov, St. Petersburg, 1900s
Illustration for the book plate of
N. A. Teffi.
2 × 2 in. (5 × 5 cm.)

15
Unknown artist, St. Petersburg, no date
Poster advertising the
Theatre of Miniatures.
40 × 28¾ in. (100 × 71 cm.)

15

16

17

16
Telyakovsky, Moscow, no date.
Poster for 'Equestrian Competitions'.
31¼ × 43¼ in. (78 × 108 cm.)

17
Unknown artist, St. Petersburg, 1900s
Poster for the Artists' Ball, detail.
25½ × 24½ in. (64 × 61 cm.)

18
N. Vasilyev, St. Petersburg, 1901
Poster for the Emperor Nicholas I's
Institute of Civil Engineers, advertising
a ball for 7 February 1901.
41½ × 29¼ in. (104 × 73 cm.)

18

19

20

19
N. N. Gerardov, St. Petersburg, 1901
Poster for the Fairy-tale Ball.
40¾ × 15½ in. (102 × 39 cm.)

20
N. Prodberesky, St. Petersburg, no date
Poster for a ball.
38 × 17½ in. (95 × 44 cm.)

21
Unknown artist, St. Petersburg, 1902
Poster for a ball.
30¾ × 22½ in. (77 × 56 cm.)

21

24

22
Ya. Ponomarenko, Moscow, 1910
Poster for the Odessa Exhibition of
Industrial Design.
49½ × 30½ in. (124 × 76.5 cm.)

23
Ya. Kekusheva, Moscow, 1897
Poster for an exhibtion of theatre bills at
the Stroganov High School.
74¾ × 26½ in. (187 × 66 cm.)

24
Unknown artist, St. Petersburg, 1904
Wrapper for a chocolate filled with nut
cream, one of a series.
5¼ × 3½ in. (13 × 8.5 cm.)

25
Ya. Ya. Belzen, St. Petersburg, 1900
Poster for the International Exhibition
of Ceramics.
44 × 44 in. (110 × 110 cm.)

26
Unknown artist, St. Petersburg, 1900s
Poster for the 'World of Music' Exhibition.
38 × 23½ in. (95 × 59 cm.)

25

26

27

Unknown artist
Polytype from a catalogue advertising the
'Palmyra' typeface, with illustrations,
from the Leman type-foundry.

27

28

F. Zakharov, Moscow, 1914
Poster for the All-Russian League for the
Campaign against Tuberculosis.
37½ × 28½ in. (94 × 71 cm.)

29

Unknown artist (initials given, N. G.),
St. Petersburg, 1910
Poster for '20 April – White Flower Day:
Help Fight Consumption!'
42¾ × 32¾ in. (107 × 82 cm.)

28

29

30   31

32

30
Unknown artist, St. Petersburg, no date
Poster advertising 'Pavlovsk Station.
Roller Skating Rink. Cinema'.
41½ × 27½ in. (104 × 69 cm.)

31
Unknown artist, Moscow, 1907
Café price-list of D.I. Philippov, Supplier
by Appointment to the Imperial Families.
Philippov was the best-known owner of
bakeries in Moscow. True Muscovites still
refer to the largest of his former shops as
the 'Philippovskaya'.
13½ × 5½ in. (34 × 14 cm.)

32
Unknown artist, Moscow, no date
Packet for 'Bis' *papirosi* (Russian
cigarettes with a cardboard mouthpiece).

33
Unknown artist, Kiev, no date
Poster advertising 'Night *blini*'. Blini are
thin pancakes, a traditional Russian
dish, eaten especially at Shrovetide,
usually with *smetana*
(a kind of soured cream).
25½ × 28¾ in. (64 × 72 cm.)

34
K.V. Izenberg, St. Petersburg, 1905
Poster for an exhibition of the Society of
Houseplant and Aquarium Enthusiasts.
27½ × 12¾ in. (69 × 32 cm.)

35
Unknown artist, Kazan, 1902
Poster advertising macaroni, a
product from the firm of the
'Heirs of V.Ya. Ustinov in Kazan:
established 1858'.
22 × 10½ in. (55 × 26 cm.)

33

34

35

36

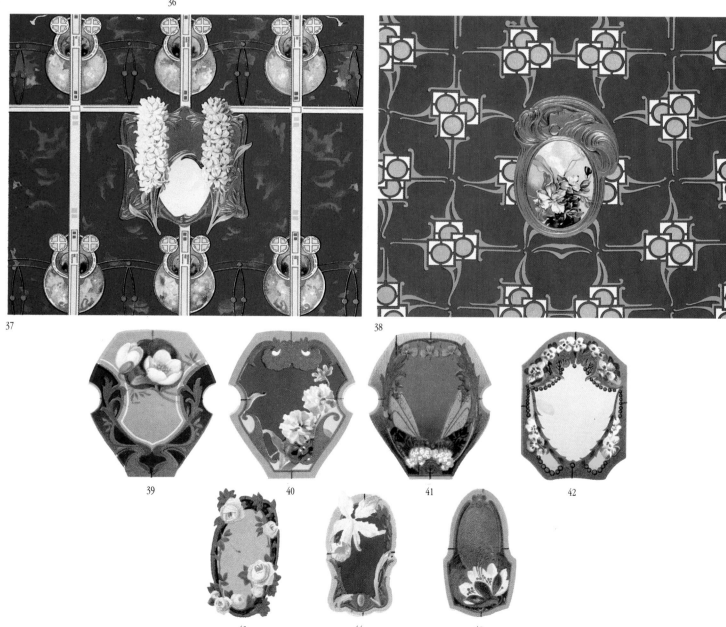

37   38

39   40   41   42

43   44   45

36
M. Belsky (?) Moscow, 1900s
Soap wrapper, prototype.
5¾ × 7½ in. (14.5 × 18.5 cm.)

37
M. Belsky (?), Moscow, 1900s
Soap wrapper, prototype.
7 × 7½ in. (17.5 × 19 cm.)

38
M. Belsky (?) Moscow, 1900s
Soap wrapper, prototype.
7¼ × 9½ in. (18 × 23.5 cm.)

39/42
M. Belsky (?) Moscow, 1900s
Perfume labels, prototype.
length 1¾ in. (4.7cm.)

43/45
M. Belsky (?) Moscow, 1900s
Perfume labels, prototypes.
length 1½ in. (4.2 cm.)

46/47
M. Belsky, Moscow, 1900s
Perfume labels, complete set, prototypes.
lengths 1 in. (2.5 cm.)
and 7 in. (17.9 cm.)

48
M. Belsky (?), Moscow 1900s
Perfume label, prototype.
length 1½ in. (4.2 cm.)

49/54
M. Belsky (?), Moscow 1900s
Perfume labels, prototypes.
length 1¾ in. (4.6 cm.)

55/60
M. Belsky (?), Moscow 1900s
Perfume labels, trial prints
length 2½ in. (6.4 cm.)

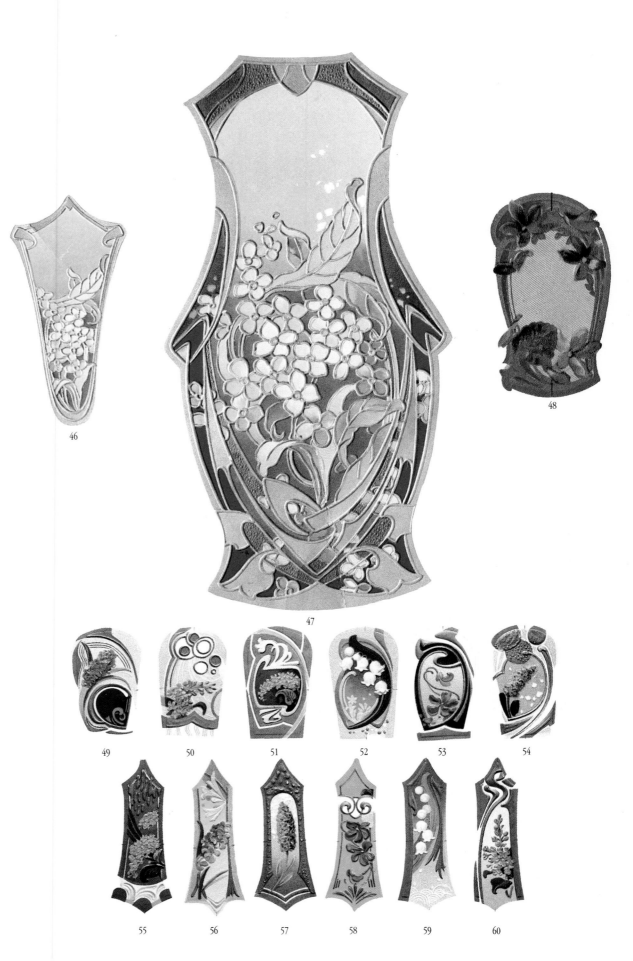

46

47

48

49   50   51   52   53   54

55   56   57   58   59   60

61

62

63

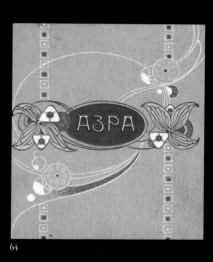

64

65

66

61
Unknown artist, St. Petersburg, 1904
Poster advertising 'Milda' *papirosi*.
11 × 18½ in. (27.5 × 46 cm.)

62
Unknown artist, Kharkov, 1913
Wrapper for 'Flora' (a sweet), original.
3¼ × 2½ in. (8 × 6.5 cm.)

63
Unknown artist, Moscow, 1900s
Label for *Snezhok* ('snowball')
a face-powder, prototype.
5¾ × 5¾ in. (14.5 × 14.5 cm.)

64
Unknown artist, Kharkov, no date
Wrapper for 'Azra' (a sweet), original.
3¾ × 3½ in. (9.5 × 8.5 cm.)

65
Unknown artist, St. Petersburg, 1903
Box for 'Moderne' toffees.
9¾ × 11¼ in. (24.5 × 28 cm.)

66
Unknown artist, St. Petersburg/Moscow,
no date
Polytype in Russian Art Nouveau from a
catalogue of Leman typefaces.

67
Unknown artist, Moscow, no date
Cover of booklet entitled 'Instructions for
the use of the most popular perfumes and
cosmetics from the firm of V.K. Ferrein.'
8 × 8½ in. (20 × 21 cm.)

68
M. Belsky (?), Moscow, 1900s
Labels for *Rezeda* ('mignonette'),
a set of perfumes from the firm
of Ralle, prototypes.
length 5½ × 2¼ in. (13.6 × 5.6 cm.)

67

НАСТАВЛЕНІЕ
КЪ ПОЛЬЗОВАНІЮ
НАИБОЛѢЕ УПОТРЕБИТЕЛЬНЫМИ
ПАРФЮМЕРНЫМИ и КОСМЕТИЧЕС-
КИМИ СРЕДСТВАМИ

Товарищества
В.К. ФЕРРЕЙНъ
Москва.

68

69

70

71

72

73

74

69
Unknown artist, St. Petersburg, no date
Wrapper for 'Konfetti' toffees.
3½ × 2 in. (8.5 × 7.5 cm.)

70
Unknown artist, St. Petersburg, 1903
Wrapper for *Fistashkovaya*
(pistachio) toffees.
3¼ × 2½ in. (8 × 6 cm.)

71/73
Unknown artist, St. Petersburg, 1900s
Series of wrappers for *Stilnaya*
('stylish') toffees.
3 × 3½ in. (7.5 × 8.5 cm.)

74
Unknown artist, St. Petersburg, 1903
Wrapper for *Rusalka* ('mermaid') toffees.
3 × 3½ in. (7.5 × 8.5 cm.)

75/76
Unknown artist, no date
Sweet wrappers, originals.
3½ × 3½ in. (8.5 × 8.5 cm.)

77/78
Unknown artist, no date
Sweet wrappers, originals.
2¾ × 3¼ in. (7 × 8 cm.)

79/80
Unknown artist, no date
Sweet wrappers, originals.
2¾ × 2¾ in. (7 × 7 cm.)

75

76

77

78

79

80

МІРЪ ИСКУССТВА.

2

3

THE WORLD OF ART GROUP

This chapter deals with a group of artists who formed a society of their own. They were all living in St. Petersburg during the *moderne* period – and this was no mere biographical coincidence. Alexandre Benois, Konstantin Somov, Lev (Léon) Bakst, Yevgeny Lansere, Mstislav Dobuzhinsky and Sergei Diaghilev did indeed live in a world of art. They painted, organized exhibitions, designed books and magazines, worked as critics, researchers and collectors of art, and made splendid contributions to theatrical set and costume design; finally, they produced their own journal – *World of Art* – and went on to organize exhibitions in its name. Those associated with this journal became known to their contemporaries, and to history, as the *miriskusniki*: the World of Art artists.

There was an element of fate in the emergence of the World of Art group. Four of its founding members – Benois, Somov, Walter Nuvel and Dmitri Filosofov – went to school together, in the same class at the private, upper middle-class May College in St.Petersburg. The class leader, Benois, gathered a group of fellow-students around him who met at his home to discuss matters of interest and take turns in reading papers. All sorts of subjects intrigued them, including music, theatre, literature, painting and theology. This schoolboy 'society for self-education' – the 'Nevsky Pickwickians', as they called themselves – brought together a group of versatile and talented young men with a common desire to explore world culture.

Their active friendship continued through their student years. All graduated from the Faculty of Law at St. Petersburg University, with the exception of Somov, who studied at the St. Petersburg Academy of Fine Arts. He and Benois, who were both to become professional painters, came from families prominent in the artistic intelligentsia. The two grew up surrounded by art and culture: Benois was the son of a distinguished St. Petersburg architect, Nikolai Benois, while Somov's father, Sergei, was a famous art historian and Curator of the Imperial Hermitage Museum.

The Benois family produced another of the World of Art group: Yevgeny Lansere, Alexandre's nephew but his junior by only a few years. Lansere also became a painter and played the major role in the design of the journal.

Sergei Diaghilev, a cousin of Dmitri Filosofov, joined Benois' circle at university in St. Petersburg, where he arrived in 1890 to study law. It was Diaghilev who was entirely responsible for the public

1
Léon Bakst, 1902
Cover for the journal, *World of Art*,
nos. 9-10.
9½ × 6¾ in. (24 × 17 cm.)

2
Yevgeny Lansere, 1903
Cover for *World of Art* (detail).
4½ × 6¼ in. (11.2 × 15.7 cm.)

3

3
Alexandre Benois, 1902
Vignette accompanying an article,
'Florence', by V. Rozanov, in
World of Art, no. 12.
4¼ × 6¾ in. (10.5 × 17 cm.)

4
Alexandre Benois, 1902
Vignette for 'Florence'.
4½ × 6¾ in. (11 × 17 cm.)

impact of the World of Art group. Blessed with an inexhaustible energy, Diaghilev was a true man of action – innovator, organizer and natural leader. It was his energy that fuelled all the enterprises undertaken by the group. When contemporaries talked of the *World of Art* journal they called it 'Diaghilev's journal'; when exhibitions were discussed, they were 'Diaghilev's exhibitions', and later the Ballets Russes in Paris was known as 'Diaghilev's Ballet'. The significance of his role in Russian and European culture during the first quarter of the twentieth century is due to a happy combination of his social activity, the breadth and sophistication of his artistic taste and an extraordinary instinct for all that was new in art.

The World of Art group first stepped into the artistic arena in 1898, when Diaghilev organized an exhibition of Russian and Finnish painters. This first exhibition included all those artists from St. Petersburg and Moscow who were to form the bedrock support of the World of Art movement. The end of the same year saw the first issue of the new journal, on whose cover the words *World of Art* appeared for the very first time. It was edited by Diaghilev and financed by two patrons already familiar to us, Savva Mamontov and Princess Tenisheva. Within the space of a year, however, their subsidies ceased. For four years the journal subsisted on state funds, until financial crisis overtook the country and the journal was left without resources. It published its last issue in 1904.

Eighty-four numbers of the journal and five annual art exhibitions were produced in a relatively brief period of intense activity which launched the group into the very centre of Russia's artistic life. These few years were sufficient to establish the aesthetic credo of the World of Art group and the creative individuality of its members, who were now independent, mature artists in their thirties. The last occasion on which the group came into the public eye was during the triumphant 'Saisons Russes' organized by Diaghilev in Paris from 1909 on, where they were responsible for the design of all the ballet and opera productions – until, eventually, Diaghilev's legendary eye for the new led him to alienate himself from his Russian associates by giving preference to young artists of the French avant-garde. Diaghilev was to remain in France to become an integral part of that country's culture, to which he devoted his later years; and, with good reason, Parisians have immortalized him by giving his name to one of the city's squares.

The unique character of the World of Art movement and the work it produced was largely determined by a single factor: it was conceived and led by men of wide education and culture. Their artistic outlook could have been summarized as follows:

1. The World of Art is seen as a synthesis of all the arts, a world created by artists of universal talents.

2. The World of Art may be comprehended by educated people. Artists are not only themselves involved in cultural life but also active in the artistic education of others.

3. The World of Art is an autonomous world, a world in itself. Its artists are apolitical and indifferent even to the burning issues of the day.

4

4. The World of Art has no boundaries of time or place. The artist is not prejudiced; he is familiar with the history of art and is at home in any culture that he finds congenial.

How was all this translated into reality? The World of Art artists were highly versatile and worked in the fields of painting, graphics and stage design, though of course all had their various preferences. Thus, Somov favoured painting and graphics; Bakst was more inclined to theatre; while Dobuzhinsky and the younger Ivan Bilibin concentrated on graphics. Perhaps only Benois, the theorist of the movement, shared his energies equally among all his activities as visual artist, art critic and scholar. He was the leading critic of the *World of Art* journal, and later, from 1908 to 1917, wrote a regular column entitled 'Artistic Letters' for the magazine *Rech* (Speech). He created a whole series of paintings and book illustrations, and also designed productions for the Moscow Art Theatre and Diaghilev's Ballets Russes.

The World of Art group were at their most brilliant in book and theatre design, both fields in which the pictorial arts engage with other branches of art, and where versatility and imagination are required from the artist. In book and theatre design alike, the artistic effect derives from the correlation between a visual interpretation and the literary or theatrical fabric of the work: a synthesis of the arts, in fact. It was precisely at such conjunctures that the members of the group came into their own.

Their life was indivisible from the literary and theatrical culture on which they were nourished, and which they served with love and dedication. They reserved their most passionate admiration for the theatre. Life unfolding on a stage and spiritualized by the beauty of singing, gesture and decor was an embodiment of that very World of Art that symbolized for them the meaning of existence. The theatre was a world apart, where fantasy and reality merged into one. They themselves, in their theatrical work, strove to transform the stage into a realm of sheer beauty. The supreme example of this theatre of beauty, at once intricate and overwhelming, is perhaps the Russian ballet, as it was presented to Parisian audiences by Diaghilev.

The unashamed cult of theatre in Benois's circle inevitably left its imprint on all the activities of the World of Art. All those elements that make up the concept of 'theatre' – elevated ideas, magic and alienation, truth and fantasy, the rejection of the mundane – characterized all the rest of their work, and most especially their graphic design.

Most of the members of the group were particularly gifted in the graphic field, to which they turned unanimously and with such enthusiasm that within a few short years at the beginning of the century they had raised its standards in Russia to unprecedented heights. The first images that come to mind when we think of the World of Art are those of elegant vignettes and elaborate drawings.

Whatever they designed – from books, magazines and posters to theatre programmes and envelopes for visiting cards – their intention was to create a thing of beauty. Their conception of book and magazine design embraced the cover, decorative titles and initials, pictorial motifs, type ornaments and the typefaces themselves. Decorative objects and forms – such as flowers, ribbons, garlands, vases and more flowers – were used in the composition of countless beautiful vignettes; critics often described the World of Art group as the masters of vignette, and someone even coined the term 'vignettists'.

By publishing a journal of their own, they were enabled to put their ideas into practice. *World of Art* was the very first illustrated art journal to be produced in Russia; in the process they explored their potential, developed their graphic styles and matured into professionals. All the graphic artists of the group participated in the development of an image for their publication which, together with the many books and magazines for which they were later responsible, pioneered the principles of modern professional design. With *World of Art,* Russian graphic design came of age and acquired a personality and idiom of its own.

The editors took particular care over standards of production. For the first time, Russian artists were involved in discussing and consciously selecting the paper and typefaces for a magazine, and deciding on the techniques of reproduction most appropriate to the character of their original drawings and other designs. They chose their printers with care and kept close watch on the quality of the work.

They were also the first in Russia to discover and establish a number of basic laws of graphic design. Artists set out to co-ordinate their work with the typeface selected, and the whole development of the magazine's collective graphic style was based on the principle of the two-dimensionality of the printed page. The World of Art style employs a symbolic and metaphorical language of line and plane that shuns illusionism and uses stylized drawing to create a subtle interplay of black and white. One early historian and passionate supporter of the group, Sergei Makovsky, defined its style: 'While leaving to painting and the other "major" arts all the reality of this world, the embodiment of forms, real

5

colour, the chiaroscuro of relief and the illusion of perspective, this graphic art reserves to itself only that which belongs to it by right: shadows, edges, the gentle luxury of contours which are not to be found in nature, tinted patterns and the black tracery of the silhouette. In this phantasmal world, graphic art reigns supreme.'[11]

The World of Art group developed their graphic style according to a conscious and consistent plan. They were well versed in the history of art and kept themselves informed on contemporary developments. They frequently visited other European centres of culture, where they lived and worked for long periods. Many studied at studios in Munich and Paris. The World of Art brought together the first generation of artists who did not restrict their professional activities to Russian art; indeed, they were eager to compare and measure their work against all that was being done in other countries. One major reason for the existence of their journal was to satisfy an urgent need in Russian culture, and their own emergence as fully fledged artists owed a great deal to their regular perusal of such foreign art publications as *The Studio, Jugend, Simplicissimus* and *Pan.*

They hoped to give an airing in the *World of Art* journal to all they considered new and significant in national and international art. It should not be forgotten that the circle of friends that gathered round the magazine was unique in its range of interests and knowledge. As a result, the journal remained broad-minded and unprejudiced; in fact the only work to which they never reconciled themselves was that of the academic school and of the pale imitators of the Wanderers' style.

The journal's first edition featured a reproduction of Victor Vasnetsov's *Three Bogatyrs* and began the process of bringing the work produced by the Abramtsevo and Talashkino craft studios to the attention of the wider public. It also made considerable efforts to introduce Russian readers to the Art Nouveau of Western Europe. It was the first Russian publication to devote several pages to the graphic work of Aubrey Beardsley and showed great interest in the work of such German illustrators as Thomas

5
Alexandre Benois, 1906
Vignette from the journal *Golden Fleece*.
2¼ × 6¾ in. (5.4 × 17 cm.)

6
Mstislav Dobuzhinsky
Vignette from *World of Art*.
4½ × 6¾ in. (11.5 × 17 cm.)

7
A. Ostroumova-Lebedeva, 1902
Engraving from the series
'Views of St. Petersburg'.
2¾ × 6½ in. (7 × 16 cm.)

Heine, Jürgen Dietz, Adolf von Menzel and Genrich Vogeler, and of a number of Scandinavian artists. Several issues were devoted to the 1900 Paris World Exposition.

Naturally, the journal was also concerned with promoting interest in its 'own' artists, and special issues were devoted to the work of Somov, of Ostroumova and of those Moscow artists – Valentin Serov and Mikhail Vrubel among them – whose work featured constantly in the exhibitions staged by the group. Many new works by Somov, Lansere, Benois, Bakst and Bilibin were specially commissioned for *World of Art*.

As they worked on the journal and discussed future articles on the history of art and architecture, the members of the editorial team formed their own independent views of the history of Russian art. Their imagination took refuge in the past, and particularly in a cult of the eighteenth century. Its ensembles of parks and pavilions, its shrubbery and statuary, its elegant costumes, gallant cavaliers and adored ladies, with all the attendant charm of outline and grace of ceremony, utterly captivated the World of Art group. They were equally delighted by the novels, the memoirs and above all the 'divine' music of the eighteenth century.

They were also attracted by the culture of the 1830s, the era of Pushkin; and themes and motifs from the past gradually came to dominate their paintings and graphics. These retrospective obsessions became almost synonymous with the World of Art itself. Their work is easily recognizable by the themes that nourished its elaborate stylization: the era of Peter the Great and Louis XIV; eighteenth-century Russian portraits and German engravings; the book illustrations of Pushkin's day; the playful ingenuity of Fyodor Tolstoy, the artist of aristocratic country-house amusements; and the Neoclassical architecture of St. Petersburg. A contemporary wrote of their nostalgic art: 'It evokes the atmosphere of eighteenth-century prints, beadwork bookmarks, dried flowers forgotten between the pages of old volumes, the charm of dilapidated objects found in dusty corners of

out-of-the-way antique shops; of grandfather's old bureau, in whose secret drawer you suddenly discover his masonic signet-ring, his jasper seal, a tiny powder-case with a mirror and a bundle of letters lovingly tied with a ribbon.'[12]

The World of Art artists were great respecters of accuracy in their recreations of bygone styles. They flourished at a time of serious academic attention to historical traditions. Benois played a central role in the study and evaluation of eighteenth- and early nineteenth-century Russian culture. He systematically collected information on the artists of that period and produced an art-historical analysis of its major works. In *World of Art* he published one article after another in which he methodically revived a whole era in the history of Russian painting and architecture.

At much the same time, Diaghilev undertook a serious study of the work of the great eighteenth-century Russian portrait painter Dmitri Levitsky, and dispatched more than six hundred letters all over the Empire in the quest for new information about his subject. Diaghilev not only wrote a monograph on the painter, complete with a definitive catalogue of his work, but organized a World of Art campaign to popularize the portrait genre itself. One result was an exhibition of portraits, staged in 1905, which evoked a considerable response from the public. Over two thousand works by Russian and Western European painters and sculptors were shown, among them many that had been rediscovered by the organizers themselves. In the following year, the World of Art group introduced Russian art to Paris with an exhibition whose historical section included icons as well as eighteenth-century portraits.

The sum of World of Art's contribution to Russian and world culture was undoubtedly greater than that of the individual artists who were its members. As long as World of Art functioned as a coherent group, its activities attracted all the progressive artistic elements in the country. But the actual creative work of the members came to its full fruition in one field only, that of graphics.

The so-called second generation of World of Art began their artistic careers around 1910, long after the magazine itself closed down. All, including the most important – such artists as Georgi Narbut, Sergei Chekhonin and Dimitri Mitrokhin – devoted all their energies to graphic art and thus firmly established its status as a separate profession.

In May 1914, only a few weeks before the beginning of the First World War, a major international exhibition of printing and graphics, which included graphic work by all the World of Art group,was held in Leipzig. A special study, timed to coincide with this event, was published in St. Petersburg, in German, under the title *Der moderne Buchschmuck in Russland* (Modern Ornamental Book Design in Russia). This volume, which summed up the graphic activities of the group, opened with illustrations and analysis of the work of Benois, Somov, Bakst and other leading lights; it closed with an introduction to the younger members, who were also the designers of the book.

8

Konstantin Somov
Born in St. Petersburg, 1869; died in
Paris, 1939. He was the son of an
illustrious art historian and Curator of
the Hermitage. Studied at the Arts High
School of the St. Petersburg Academy of
Arts, under Vereshchagin, Chistyakov and
Repin; and at the studio of Colarossi in
Paris. He was one of the organizers of the
World of Art group and – as painter and
graphic artist – its most talented
representative. Academician from 1913.
One of the founders of the 'retrospective'
movement which was so distinctive an
aspect of the World of Art. He felt that
beauty was to be found only in the past
and derived his inspiration from the
culture of the eighteenth century. He is
sometimes known as the painter of
'rainbows and kisses'. His graphic work is
primarily in the field of book design. He
possessed great delicacy of technique; his
drawings display a sureness of line and
contour and the touch of a gifted
miniaturist. He was a talented vignettist
and his bookplates and book-covers are
notable for the charm of their designs. He
had a particular fondness for a technique
using the black silhouette.

9

11

8
Konstantin Somov, early 1900s
'The Kiss', silhouette from the
journal *Apollon*.
5¾ × 5½ in. (14.4 × 14.2 cm.)

9
Konstantin Somov, 1908
Illustration from the book
Le Livre de la Marquise.
1½ × 2¾ in. (3.5 × 7.1 cm.)

10
Konstantin Somov, 1908
Illustration from *Le Livre de la Marquise*.
2½ × 4¼ in. (6.5 × 10.5 cm.)

11
Konstantin Somov, 1907
Title page from the book *Theatre*,
published by Shipovnik.
11¼ × 7½ in. (28 × 19 cm.)

10

12
Konstantin Somov, 1899 (?)
Silhouette on writing paper.
3¼ × 2¼ in. (7.9 × 5.9 cm.)

13
Konstantin Somov, 1911
Book cover: *Cor Ardens* by
Vyacheslav Ivanov, published in
Moscow by Scorpion in 1911.
9¼ × 6½ in. (23 × 16.5 cm.)

14
Konstantin Somov, 1904
Vignette from a postcard in the series
'Days of the Week': Thursday. Published
by the Community of St. Eugenia of the
Red Cross.
5¾ × 3¾ in. (14.5 × 9.5 cm.)

15
Konstantin Somov, 1900
Cover of a theatre programme for
10 February 1900.
12 × 9½ in. (30 × 24 cm.)

12

16
Konstantin Somov, 1900
Cover of a theatre programme for
17 January 1900 (detail).
10¾ × 8 in. (27 × 20 cm.)

17
Konstantin Somov, 1911
Vignette from a postcard. Published by
the Community of St. Eugenia of the
Red Cross.
5½ × 3½ in. (14 × 9 cm.)

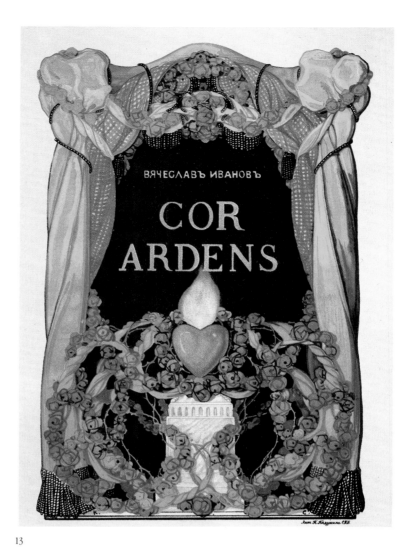

ВЯЧЕСЛАВЪ ИВАНОВЪ

COR
ARDENS

13

14

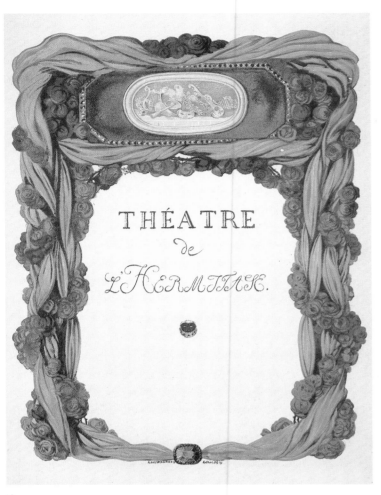

15

16

17

18
Alexandre Benois, 1899 (?)
Silhouette on writing paper.
3½ × 3½ in. (8.9 × 8.7 cm.)

19
Konstantin Somov, 1907
Cover of the book by K. Balmont,
The Fire-Bird, published in Moscow
by Scorpion in 1907.
8½ × 6¾ in. (21 × 17 cm.)

20
Konstantin Somov, 1908
'*Petit besoin*', illustration from
Le Livre de la Marquise
3½ × 1½ in. (9 × 4.2 cm.)

18

21
Konstantin Somov, 1908
'*Le Pot de Chambre*,' illustration from
Le Livre de la Marquise
2¾ × 4¼ in. (7 × 10.5 cm.)

19

20   21

Alexandre Benois
Born in St. Petersburg, 1870; died in
Paris, 1960. His family belonged to the
artistic intelligentsia. Graduated from
the Law Faculty of St. Petersburg
University and attended lectures at the
St. Petersburg Academy of Arts. Travelled
widely in Europe, living and working in
France for long periods of time. The
theorist, and one of the founders, of the
World of Art group. He was active in the
field of art education and specialized in
several fields: he was a scholar, the
author of several books on art history,
as well as the leading critic of the *World
of Art* journal; painter; and designer
for Diaghilev, the Moscow Art Theatre,
La Scala in Milan, the Comédie-Française,
etc. In graphics he owed his success as
a book-illustrator to his erudition and
unerring stylistic instinct. His work
is imbued with and inspired by his
deep knowledge and love of the past,
particularly the cultures of Russia and
Louis XIV.

22
Alexandre Benois, 1911
Illustration for *The Queen of Spades*
by Pushkin. Illumination of
chapter heading.
3¼ × 5½ in. (8 × 13.5 cm.)

23
Alexandre Benois, 1904
Card in the series 'Easter in the XVIII
Century'. 'The Old Men', detail. Published
by the Community of St. Eugenia of the
Red Cross.
5¾ × 3½ in. (14.5 × 9 cm.)

24
Alexandre Benois, 1904
'Easter in the XVIII Century':
Devochka-Pai ('the good little girl'),
detail.
5¾ × 3½ in. (14.5 × 9 cm.)

25
Alexandre Benois, 1911
Illustration for *The Queen of Spades*
by Pushkin. Chapter ending.
2¼ × 3½ in. (5.5 × 8.5 cm.)

26
Alexandre Benois, 1911
Illustration for *The Queen of Spades*.
Illumination of chapter heading.
3 × 5½ in. (7.5 × 14 cm.)

22

23

24

25

26

27

28

30

Léon Bakst (Rosenberg)
Born in Grodno, 1866; died in Paris,
1924. He attended lectures at the
St. Petersburg Academy of Arts and
continued his studies in various Paris
studios. One of the organizers of the
World of Art group and designer of its
logo. Painter, graphic artist and theatre
designer, especially for Diaghilev, where
his talent found its true home. He was
less active in graphic design, confining
himself mainly to illustrations, book-
covers and magazine sketches. He shared
with his fellow-members of the World of
Art a passion for the past, though he
alone selected antiquity as a model. His
work includes elements of Greek
mythology and classical art.

27
Léon Bakst, early 1900s
Vignette, 'Ellada'.

28
Léon Bakst, 1901
Illustration for poems by Balmont,
Sliyaniye ('Confluence') published in
World of Art.
8 × 8¾ in. (20 × 22 cm.)

29
Léon Bakst, 1906
Vignette from the journal *Golden Fleece*,
no. 4.
4¼ × 4¼ in. (10.5 × 10.5 cm.)

30
Léon Bakst, 1903
Vignette from *World of Art*, nos. 5-6,
accompanying an article entitled
'Contemporary Art'.
8 × 4 in. (20 × 10 cm.)

31
Léon Bakst, 1908
Poster for the exhibition of Russian
artists at the *Secession* in Vienna
(sketch).
19½ × 24 in. (48.8 × 60.2 cm.)

32
Léon Bakst, 1907
Card, 'My favourite poet', published by
the Community of St. Eugenia of the
Red Cross.
5½ × 3½ in. (14 × 9 cm.)

33
Léon Bakst, 1907
Frontispiece to a volume of poems by
Alexander Blok, *The Snow Mask*.
5¼ × 3½ in. (13 × 9.5 cm.)

29

31

32

33

34

34

Léon Bakst, 1907
Cover of a book: *Artistic Treasures of
Russia* (detail).
1½ × 1¼ in. (4.2 × 3.2 cm.)

35

Léon Bakst, 1899
Poster for the 'Great Dolls' Charity
Bazaar'. The proceeds helped to fund
the work of a charity for foundlings
in St. Petersburg.
28 × 40¾ in. (70 × 102 cm.)

36

Léon Bakst, 1904
Poster for 'Art cards for the Red Cross'
20¼ × 27¼ in. (51 × 68 cm.)

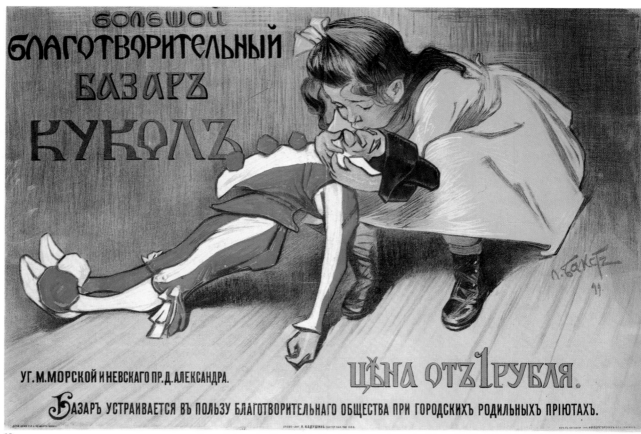

35

36

Mstislav Dobuzhinsky
Born in Novgorod, 1875; died in New York, 1957. Graduated from the Law Faculty of St. Petersburg University and studied art in Munich at the Anton Azbe school. Travelled widely in Europe and America. Member of the World of Art group. Painter, theatre designer but first and foremost a graphic artist. The theme of the city held a greater fascination for him than for most other artists. He was a master of technique and composition, preferring to work with line. He strongly influenced the development of graphics in the first quarter of the twentieth century.

39

37

37
Mstislav Dobuzhinsky, 1908
Silhouette 'Madrigal', detail, on writing paper, published by the Community of St. Eugenia of the Red Cross.
3¼ × 2½ in. (8 × 6.6 cm.)

38
Mstislav Dobuzhinsky, 1906
Colophon from the *Golden Fleece*.
1½ × 3¾ in. (4 × 9.5 cm.)

39
Mstislav Dobuzhinsky, 1912
Cover of an invitation card. The hundredth anniversary of the battle of Borodino was widely celebrated in this year.
7¼ × 8 in. (18 × 20.4 cm.)

40
Mstislav Dobuzhinsky
Cover for a book of stories and poems by Alexei Remizov.
8 × 6¼ in. (20.5 × 15.5 cm.)

41
Mstislav Dobuzhinsky, 1910
Cover for a collection of Knut Hamsun's work.
8 × 6¼ in. (20.5 × 15.5 cm.)

42
Mstislav Dobuzhinsky, 1910
Cover for a programme of symphony concerts conducted by Sergei Kussevitsky.

40

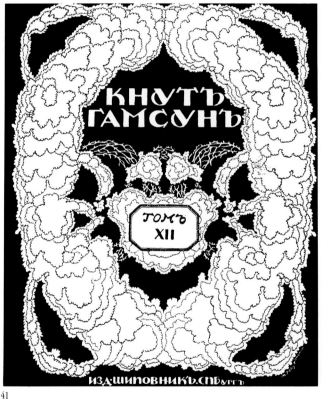

41

38

42

43

45

44

Nikolai Remizov

Born in St. Petersburg, 1887. The date of his death is not known. Frequently signed his work 'Re-mi'. Studied at the St. Petersburg Academy of Arts in the studio of Kardovsky. He was the most productive of the artists associated with the journals *Satiricon* and *New Satiricon*, where he helped to raise the standards of Russian satirical drawing. He is also known for his illustrations and posters.

Yevgeny Lansere

Born in Pavlovsk (near St. Petersburg), 1875; died in Moscow, 1946. Grew up among the Benois family, studied at the Drawing School of the Society for the Encouragement of the Arts in St. Petersburg and later in various Paris studios. Member of the World of Art group. Academician from 1912. Worked in book design, painting and theatre design. He was director of the St. Petersburg China Factories between 1912 and 1915. He was a very productive graphic artist and the most active of the designers of the *World of Art* journal.

43
Nikolai Remizov, 1911
Poster advertising the journal *Apollon*.
23¼ × 27½ in. (58 × 69 cm.)

44
Yevgeny Lansere, 1909
Vignette from the cover of I. Grabar's
History of Russian Art.
2½ × 2¼ in. (6.5 × 6 cm.)

45
Yevgeny Lansere, early 1900s
Logo for the Exhibitions of
Contemporary Art.

46

47

48

46
Yevgeny Lansere, early 1900s
Illustration from Alexandre Benois' book,
Tsarskoe Selo (detail).

47
Yevgeny Lansere, 1911
Poster for a 'Historical Exhibition
of Architecture'.
38 × 33¼ in. (95 × 83 cm.)

48
Nikolai Remizov, 1903
Poster for the 'Permanent Exhibition
of Contemporary Art'.
38¾ × 34¾ in. (97 × 87 cm.)

49
Yevgeny Lansere, 1904
Illustration for Balmont's poem
'Hymn to the Sun', published in
World of Art, no. 12.
4½ × 6½ in. (11 × 16 cm.)

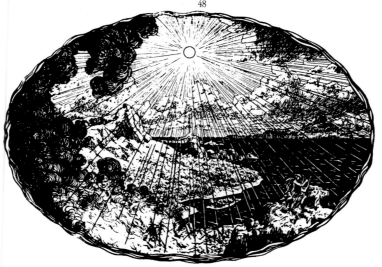

49

Georgi Narbut

Born on the Narbutovka estate, Chernigov province, 1886; died in Kiev, 1920. He had no formal artistic education. Naturally gifted as a graphic artist, in his youth he was drawn to and imitated the work of Bilibin. Together with Chekhonin and Mitrokhin he was among the finest of the younger World of Art generation of graphic artists. He was particularly attracted by stylization and his own work progressed through several styles, including the 'Bilibin', 'Silhouette', 'Chinese' and 'Heraldic'. He was a master of many different techniques and did virtuoso work with typefaces. He completed a vast number of commissions during his short lifetime, among them book-covers, illustrations, sketches, fly-leaf drawings, designs for wallpaper and textiles, book plates and typefaces.

50/52
Georgi Narbut, 1910s
Vignettes (details).

53
Georgi Narbut, 1916
Title page of the journal *Apollon*.
8½ × 6½ in. (21 × 16.5 cm.)

54
Georgi Narbut, 1912
Illustration from an edition of
Krylov's *Fables*.
1¾ × 6¾ in. (4.5 × 17 cm.)

53

54

55

56

55/56
Georgi Narbut, 1913
Illustrations for Hans Christian
Andersen's story 'The High Jumpers'.
7½ × 6½ in. (19 × 16 cm.)

57
Georgi Narbut, 1912
Title-page of Krylov's *Fables*.
6½ × 6 in. (16.7 × 15 cm.)

57

58
Sergei Chekhonin
Type-face initial.

59/60
Georgi Narbut, 1907
Envelopes for visiting cards, published by
the Community of St. Eugenia of the
Red Cross.

61
Léon Bakst, 1902
Cover of a theatre programme for
'Contemporary Ballet'.
9¼ × 6½ in. (23 × 16 cm.)

58

59

60

62
Unknown artist, St. Petersburg, 1903
Invitation: 'The Mayor of St. Petersburg
has the honour to request your kind
attendance at a sailing and rowing
regatta on 18 May 1903 at 2 pm on
the occasion of the two-hundredth
anniversary of the founding
of St. Petersburg.'
5½ × 9½ in. (14 × 23.5 cm.)

63
A. Golovin, Moscow, 1903
Theatre programme cover.
9½ × 7½ in. (24 × 19 cm.)

64
A. Golovin, Moscow, 1902
Theatre programme cover.
11¾ × 10½ in. (29.5 × 26 cm.)

65
Unknown artist. No date.
Envelope for visiting card.

61

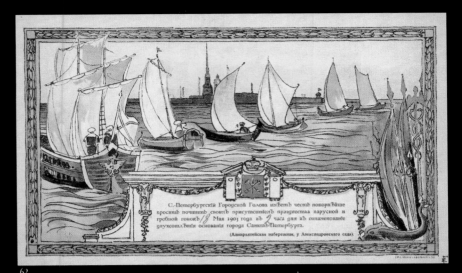

62

63

64

65

СРЕДСТВА отъ НАСѢКОМЫХЪ:
АНТИПАРАЗИТЪ,
ДАЛМАТСКАЯ РОМАШКА,
АРАГАЦЪ.
ЖИДКОСТЬ отъ КЛОПОВЪ и
ТАРАКАНОВЪ,
ЖИДКОСТЬ отъ МОЛИ,
ДУХИ отъ КОМАРОВЪ.
СОБСТВЕННЫЯ ПРОИЗВЕДЕНІЯ
МОСК. АКЦ. ОБЩ.
К. ЭРМАНСЪ и Ко.
ВЪ МОСКВѢ.
ЛИТ. Ю. КИРСТЕНЪ. ПРЕЕМН. БР. МЕНЕРТЪ МОСКВА.

1

2

4

COMMERCIAL GRAPHICS

The rapid growth of printing activity at the turn of the century brought with it the need to advertise the industry's wares and to publicize its achievements. In 1895, the First All-Russian Printing Exhibition was held in St. Petersburg; it was an impressive display which remained open for several months from noon to midnight daily, and was accompanied by the publication of thirty-four issues of a review that contained detailed information about all sections of the exhibition and described the most modern photomechanical processes in printing, an industry which stood on the threshold of the greatest revolution in its history. The organizers described their aim as follows: 'We wish to present the current situation in printing . . . that is, to demonstrate this greatest of all forces serving the education and development of mankind.'[13]

The 1895 exhibition was a fusion of art and industrial design. All the major national publishing houses and examples of their output were well represented, in addition to the whole range of printing technology, from the most modern equipment available to the paint used for gilding page-edges. One of the most striking exhibits was a working rotary press which printed the magazine *Niva* before the public's very eyes in a demonstration combining the swiftest and most modern technology with the most popular magazine in Russia (its circulation was 115,000 in 1891 and 235,000 by 1900). The *Review of the First All-Russian Printing Exhibition* carried a photograph of 'The printing of *Niva* on the rotary press in the presence of His Imperial Majesty.'[14]

One issue of the review described the Dalmatov collection, included in the exhibition, as 'a most remarkable assemblage of ancient examples of elaborate ornament, embroidery and lace.'[15] It consisted of 3,500 pieces and weighed no less than 43 poods (704 kg or 1,550 pounds). This reflected yet another example of the enthusiastic provision of a properly documented historical resource for artists working in the 'Russian Style'. Several years earlier, in 1889, a book had appeared (designed in 'Russian Style' by Ivan Ropet himself) whose title, beautifully lettered in ornate calligraphy, spoke for itself: 'Russian Embroidery Work by K. Dalmatov, using coloured silks, on satin for soft furnishings and on linen for door and window valances, intended for the decoration of the Russian Terem [tower-chamber] in the Danish Royal Park at Fredenberg in 1889. Patterns taken by K. Dalmatov from his extensive collection of ancient examples of Russian folk needlework from the provinces of Moscow, Novgorod, Tver and Yaroslavl.'

1
Unknown artist, Moscow, no date
Leaflet advertising insecticide
products from the Moscow
firm of K. Ermans & Co.
14 × 10¼ in. (35 × 25.5 cm.)

2
Unknown artist
One rouble banknote.
3¼ × 5¾ in. (8.3 × 14.3 cm.)

3   4

The 1895 printing exhibition concentrated on books and periodicals: a reflection of the overriding importance that the Russian intelligentsia attached to education, and to books in particular. The journals, exhibitions and catalogues of the day vividly evoke this side of graphic design; but all the visual aspects of the printing world were closely interconnected, and familiarity with one will help us to understand much about the others. Thus, although publications might have different purposes, they shared the same publishers and printing-houses. Commercial graphics, such as posters, advertisements, and other ephemera, shared with books and magazines the typefaces and ornaments that their creators took from the same catalogues; their graphic language was limited by available printing techniques; they displayed certain fashionable similarities in style; and they were frequently the work of the same designers.

By the end of the first decade of the twentieth century, the print industry had acquired considerable self-confidence and no longer felt the need to trumpet its importance or justify its existence. From 1908 onwards, annual 'Exhibitions of the Printed Word' were organized whose aim was 'to display everything produced by the Russian printing industry in the current year'.[16] Accordingly, although its largest section was devoted to 'Upbringing and Education' – students at all levels and their teachers still being the main book-buyers in Russia – the first Exhibition of the Printed Word included not only books and periodicals but posters, postcards, maps and calendars. The last of these exhibitions was staged in 1913; then came the war.

In 1898, its first year of publication, the magazine *Art and Industrial Design* led a campaign to stimulate commercial graphic art. Every issue contained an announcement of some competition organized by the editors for 'best designs for postcards', 'decorative designs in national style based on motifs of flora and fauna from any region of the Empire', 'best design for magazine cover', 'best design for titling, ornamental initials and tailpieces', 'best ornamental design for visiting-card envelopes' and so on.

Articles reporting on these competitions gradually defined the broad contours of the emerging profession of graphic design. This was almost the first time that the requirements to be met by applied

3
Unknown artist
Five rouble banknote.
6¼ × 3¾ in. (15.7 × 9.7 cm.)

4
Unknown artist
Ten rouble banknote.
7 × 4¼ in. (17.6 × 10.5 cm.)

5
Unknown artist
25 rouble banknote, bearing a portrait of
Emperor Alexander III.
4¼ × 7 in. (10.7 × 17.8 cm.)

graphic art had actually been formulated: 'The correspondence between a design and its specific intention is an essential element in the art of industrial design. Competitors seriously hoping to attract the judges' approval should concentrate on the task in hand and not be tempted into irrelevant digressions.'[17] Another revealing comment: 'Before starting work on a design, the artist should acquaint himself, at least in general terms, with all technical aspects of its possible future reproduction.'[18]

Reporting on the competition for a cover design, the editors somewhat belatedly expressed their own design creed in these terms: 'What is required of a cover? First and foremost, a clear, easily legible and even catchy typeface for the title or titles. If there are to be any decorative motifs or drawings on the cover, these should be distinct, intelligible and arranged with such sense of proportion and harmony of tone as to be in tune with the spirit of the publication; finally, they should not present undue technical complications for mass reproduction in print.'[19]

All the editorial comments expressed strong concern at the great number of imitative and unoriginal entries to the competitions: '. . . we give notice for the future that all competitors who are satisfied with crude copies of various more or less well-known foreign examples will find their entries summarily rejected. Serious workers in this field should always aim for original design. It is high time to cease the slavish imitation of foreign material.'[20]

Similar themes were widely echoed in comment on the new art of industrial design. A report on an annual competition organized by the Imperial Society for the Encouragement of the Arts complained: 'Many entries to the industrial design section made an unhappy impression on the judges. Cliché, deficiency of taste, fear of anything original and unusual – these qualities were far too much in evidence. Composition was all too often reduced to compilation, i.e. to the most undesirable and lifeless element of art.'[21]

The editors of *Art and Industrial Design* constantly challenged artists to be innovators: 'Can it really be the case that our young people are not attracted by the idea of creative work? Are they really unable to create anything truly original or individual?' This cry of despair was followed by a clarification of the magazine's own position, which reflected the views of many contemporary Russian artists: 'Our national and natural heritage is surely rich enough to provide the artist with inspiration; we have but to cast our eyes over the folk art of the past to be convinced that it is the only sure foundation for the creation of a truly Russian tradition of industrial design.'[22]

The campaign of stimulation by competition concluded with an editorial announcement placed on the last page of the fourth issue of *Art and Industrial Design* for 1901. It ended as follows: 'Finding ourselves unable to give currency to simple-minded and eclectic imitations, or to encourage designs in

5

a totally decadent style, the editors are unfortunately obliged to suspend this venture until a more apposite time.'

It was at this point, in October 1901, that the first issue of a new journal, *The Art of Printing*, appeared. The publisher and editor was Ivan Leman, a leading member of the family typefounding firm of O. I. Leman, which, along with the St. Petersburg branch of the Berlin firm Berthold & Co., was the largest of its kind in Russia. From the end of the nineteenth century until the 1917 revolution, these two enterprises had an enormous influence on the development of Russian typographic design. The new magazine's editorial board expressed its intentions in these terms: 'We shall use our publication to inform our readers – as fairly and fully as possible – of all the new and significant developments that occur in the contemporary techniques of the art of printing.'[23]

This journal survived for two years; Imperial Russia was not to see its like again. *The Art of Printing* was a professional publication entirely devoted to graphic design. It did indeed fulfil its mission to describe all that was 'new and significant'. It contained articles about publishers and the

6

latest printing technology, covered exhibitions and provided a diary of professional events. Every issue included examples of current jobbing work (which indirectly advertised the publisher's own typefounding business). Each issue displayed a different cover, featuring varied decorative designs which were basically *moderne* in style.

What were the main causes of the gradual improvement in the quality of professional standards of typesetting, printing and graphic design? They certainly included the regular appearance of catalogues of the typefaces and decorative patterns available from Russian typefoundries; and the birth of numerous, if short-lived, journals and magazines that specialized in printing technique and were intended primarily for compositors. Somewhat later, little books appeared in the same vein; one has the promising title, *A Talk on the Composition of Titling and This, That and the Other*. Its equally appealing contents consist of practical advice to young compositors, explaining why 'such a seemingly simple matter as the Composition of Titling has caused such headaches among many of the foremost European printers.'[24]

The turn of the century saw revolutionary technological changes that transformed the subsequent development of the industry. Above all, printing-houses mastered photomechanical printing processes. As recently as the 1890s, all mass reproduction had been done from wood engravings: that is, paintings and photographs were first turned into wood blocks, cut by hand, from which the printing itself was done. The printing of illustrations by this means was a highly labour-intensive and costly process, not to mention the inevitable distortion of the original image that was entailed.

6
Unknown artist
100 rouble banknote, bearing a portrait of Catherine the Great.
4¾ × 10¼ in. (12.2 × 25.8 cm.)

7
Unknown artist
500 rouble banknote, bearing a portrait of Peter the Great.
5 × 11 in. (12.6 × 27.3 cm.)

It took about ten years for printers to switch from the old methods to the new photomechanical techniques. This resulted in an unprecedented dissemination of photographic reproductions as well as the appearance of a new type of publication, the weekly photo magazine.

The new process dramatically transformed the appearance of printed graphics. The ability to reproduce artists' originals with photographic precision enabled them to use a much broader range of graphic language in their work. The generation of artists associated with the World of Art was the first whose graphic output could be mass-reproduced using this revolutionary technique; and because of it they were able to employ the elaborate line-drawing and mixed media without which their unique graphic style could never have arisen.

The transfer to the new technology was vividly reflected in the pages of the various publications. The first issue of *Art and Industrial Design* for the year 1900 carried the announcement that it contained eighteen photographs, 'two in collotype, two in colour and one by the new three-colour printing method'. In 1903, the year's first number of *World of Art* bore on its title-page, designed by Konstantin

7

Somov, the following text: '28 Autotypes, 3 Chromolithographs. 3 Collotypes. Heliogravure.' And so forth.

Printing, photography and graphic design henceforward entered a threefold union in which they were mutually involved and dependent. And so, just as exhibitions of the printed word featured printing technology, photographic exhibitions covered the application of photography to printing. We can only marvel at the breadth of interest displayed by the organizers of the International Photographic Exhibition mounted in St. Petersburg in 1903, which included the following sections: scientific photography; art photography; photomechanical printing processes; photographic literature; technical applications of photography; and the photographic industry. Reviews of the next International Photographic Exhibition (in Moscow in 1908) drew special attention to the large numbers of high-quality reproductions printed 'in natural colours', as they were described.

The illustrations in this chapter present examples of mass-produced graphic work: the design that is associated with consumer goods and their advertisement, including labels, forms of various kinds, packaging, and posters. In the early part of the twentieth century, the growth of industry and trade in Russia was accompanied by an intensive increase in advertising activity; as the century wore on, this was to become the main branch of graphic design.

In the field of advertising graphics we detect traces of many styles, including versions of Russian Style, *moderne* and eclecticism. However, most are composed in a kind of 'commercial style', a timeless, spontaneous and somehow cosmopolitan manner – traditionally associated with the design of goods for sale – which continues the vivid style of nineteenth-century signwriting and labels. These compositions typically feature elaborately calligraphic letter forms, an abundance of ornamentation, and a pursuit of an opulent, splendid effect.

The examples of advertising contained in this book tell us, of course, about the goods that were bought and sold at the time. We come across firms familiar to Russian eyes through advertisements in Soviet times, when pre-revolutionary enterprises were given new names: after 1917, 'Triangle' became 'Red Triangle', and 'Einem' became 'Red October'. Above all, however, these advertisements reveal something of the flourishing commercial life of pre-revolutionary Russia: all the mercantile activity that so colourfully prevailed at the famous Nizhny Novgorod Trade Fair, held every year on the banks of the Volga.

8

9

8
Unknown artist
Three rouble banknote.
4 × 6 in. (9.9 × 15.3 cm.)

9
P. Ostashov, Moscow, 1884
Advertisement for the Maria Vasilevna
Sadomovaya factory, the 'foremost
manufactory of knitting and
embroidery yarns'.
21½ × 28¾ in. (54 × 72 cm.)

10

10
Unknown artist, Moscow, 1872
Polytype: Moscow Polytechnical
Exhibition 1872.
Leman type-foundry

11
Unknown artist, St. Petersburg,
after 1909
Poster advertising products from
S.Kh. Randrup's factory in Omsk.
35½ × 20 in. (89 × 50 cm.)

12
Unknown artist, St. Petersburg, no date
Poster for the Weiner brewery in
Astrakhan, based on a well-known
painting by Vasnetsov entitled
'At the Crossroads'.
30½ × 20¾ in. (76 × 52 cm.)

13
Unknown artist, St. Petersburg, no date
Advertising poster for 'A.M. Zhukov's
Soap'. Under the picture, the words read
'Bazaar at the time of Mikhail
Fedorovich' (the first Romanov tsar,
1613–1645)
20½ × 14 in. (51 × 35 cm.)

14
Unknown artist, St. Petersburg, no date
Poster advertising *Treugolnik* (triangle)
galoshes.
34 × 21½ in. (85 × 54 cm.)

11

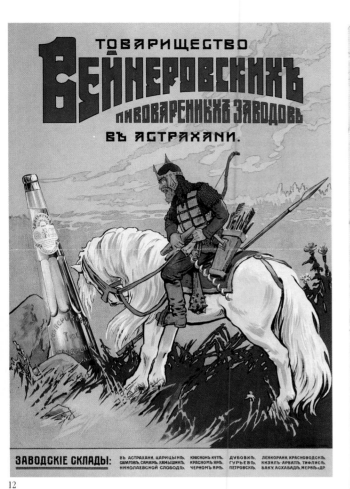

12

13

14

15

16

15
Unknown artist, Moscow, 1903
Poster: 'Tea. Tea merchants Sergei
Alexeyevich Sporov of Moscow'.
21½ × 28¾ in. (54 × 72 cm.)

16
Unknown artist, St. Petersburg, no date
Label of wrapper for cloth, from the
Alexandro-Nevsky factory of
K. Ya. Pal.
7½ × 9½ in. (18.5 × 24 cm.)

17
Unknown artist, St. Petersburg/Moscow,
no date
Polytype for the All-Russian Exhibition
of 1882. Leman type-foundry.

18
Unknown artist, St. Petersburg, no date
Poster for the Singer Sewing Machine
Company.
44½ × 27½ in. (111 × 69 cm.)

19
Unknown artist, Moscow, no date
Poster for the so-called 'Perfumery of the
Russian Boyars' – A. Ralle & Co.
42¾ × 28½ in. (107 × 71 cm.)

18

19

20

21

22

23

24

25

20
Unknown artist, Moscow, 1910
Poster for the Palm Sunday bazaar
organized by the Board of City Guardians
in aid of the poor.
22 × 13¾ in. (55 × 34.5 cm.)

21/22
Unknown artist (initials A.S.),
St. Petersburg, 1910s
Easter cards: 'Christ Has Risen!'
5½ × 3½ in. (14 × 9 cm.)

23
V. Klimenko, St. Petersburg, 1905
Easter card.
5¾ × 3½ in. (14.5 × 9 cm.)

24
Unknown artist, Moscow, 1915
Easter card: 'Christ Has Risen!'
5¾ × 3¾ in. (14 × 9.5 cm.)

25
Unknown artist, Kiev, 1915
Easter Card: 'Happy Easter' (literally,
'Congratulations at Holy Easter!')
The moral text underneath reads:
'No to drunkenness!'
3½ × 5½ in. (9 × 14 cm.)

26
Unknown artist, St. Petersburg/Moscow,
no date
Polytype from Leman type-foundry.

27
Unknown artist, St. Petersburg, no date
Poster advertising the *Burlaki* (bargees)
brand of cardboard tubes, used with
papirosi for rolling cigarettes.
29½ × 14½ in. (74 × 36 cm.)

28
Unknown artist, St. Petersburg, no date
Advertising cards for the Einem Steam
Company from a series entitled 'Views
and Characters of Old Moscow'. The
subject is 'Convicts sweeping the street in
the eighteenth century'.
2½ × 4½ in. (6.5 × 11 cm.)

29/30
Unknown artist, Moscow, no date
Advertising cards from the Einem Steam
Company from the series entitled 'Scenes
from Russian Life'. The subjects are
'Threshing in Central Russia' and 'Volga
fishermen eating lunch'.
2½ × 4½ in. (6.5 × 11 cm.)

26

27

28

29

30

31

Unknown artist, St. Petersburg, no date
Poster for the Society for the Production
and Sale of Gunpowder.
22¾ × 14¾ in. (57 × 37 cm.)

32

Unknown artist, St. Petersburg, no date
Chocolate wrapper from a series entitled
'Russian Sayings'; this one, in rhyme,
says: 'Look with your eyes but don't touch
with your hands!'
4½ × 2¼ in. (11 × 5.9 cm.)

33

Unknown artist, St. Petersburg, 1904
Poster for the A.N. Bogdanov & Co.
Tobacco Factory, St. Petersburg.
19½ × 24 in. (49 × 60 cm.)

34

Unknown artist, centre 1905, others
no date.
Wrappers for *papirosi: Kozyrniye*
('trumps'), Taras Bulba, *Duchesse*,
Volga, *Babochka* ('butterfly')
3½ × 1¾ in.; 3¾ × 1¾ in.;
3¼ × 2 in.; 3¾ × 2 in.; 3½ × 2 in.
(8.5 × 4.5 cm.; 9.5 × 4.5 cm.;
8 × 5 cm.; 9.5 × 5 cm; 9 × 5 cm.)

33

34

35

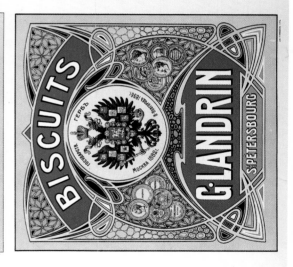

36

37

38

35
Unknown artist, Moscow, no date
Wrapper for *Kupecheskoye* (merchant)
soap.
5¼ × 4½ in. (13 × 11.5 cm.)

36
Unknown artist, St. Petersburg, no date
Wrapper for G. Landrin's
'English Biscuits'.
10¾ × 9½ in. (27 × 24 cm.)

37
Packets for *papirosi*, backs, see also no.
34 for fronts.

38
Unknown artist, St. Petersburg, no date
Chocolate wrapper in the series
'Russian Sayings': 'If you shoot at
two hares, you'll catch neither.'
(A bird in the hand...)
4½ × 3½ in. (11.5 × 9 cm.)

39
Unknown artist, St. Petersburg, 1904
Poster advertising paints, varnishes,
brushes and other products from the
Moscow firm of F. & A. Shemshurin Bros.
27½ × 14½ in. (69 × 36 cm.)

39

40

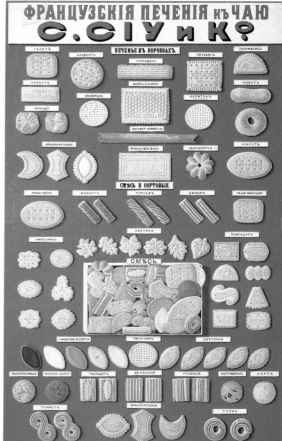

41

42

43

40
Unknown artist, Moscow, no date
Page from an advertising booklet from
the firm of Siou, with illustrations of
various biscuits.
8½ × 5½ in. (21.5 × 14.2 cm.)

41
Unknown artist, Moscow, no date
Poster for 'French tea biscuits.
S. Siou & Co.'
32 × 20½ in. (80 × 51 cm.)

42
Unknown artist, Moscow, no date
Poster: 'I.L. Ding, confectioners.
Original wrapper'.
30¼ × 18 in. (75.5 × 45 cm.)

43
Unknown artist, Moscow, no date
Chocolate wrapper from the 'Russian
Sayings' series. Saying illustrated:
'Where there's honey there's poison.'
4½ × 3½ in. (11.5 × 9 cm.)

44
Unknown artist, Moscow, no date
Poster for A. Viktorson's cardboard tubes
for *papirosi*.
27 × 16¼ in. (67.5 × 40.5 cm.)

44

45

46

47

49

48

45
Unknown artist, Moscow, no date
Label for wine No. 26 from the firm of
Ivan Alexeyevich Smirnov & Sons,
Varvarka St., Moscow.
3¼ × 4¾ in. (8 × 12 cm.)

46
Unknown artist, Moscow, no date
Label for table wine from I.A. Smirnov
of Bogorodsk.
4 × 3¼ in. (10 × 8 cm.)

47
Unknown artist, Moscow, no date
Label for wine from the Markov
Melekessky distillery, No. 23.
4½ × 3 in. (10.5 × 7.5 cm.)

48
Unknown artist, Moscow, no date
Label for Varvarka table wine from
I.A. Smirnov & Sons, illustrating
Varvarka Street, where the firm
was situated.
4 × 4½ in. (10 × 11.5 cm.)

49
Unknown artist, St. Petersburg, no date
Label for a bottle of 'Extrait d'Oranges
Ameres Blanches' Gotthard Martini,
St. Petersburg.
4¾ × 4 in. (12 × 10 cm.)

50
Unknown artist, Moscow, no date
Cover of a wine catalogue from
A. Serebryakov, trial print
11¾ × 7¾ in. (29.5 × 19.5 cm.)

51/52
Unknown artist, St. Petersburg, no date
Poster for I. Durdin's Bohemia Brewery at
Rybinsk, and detail.
36 × 20½ in. (90 × 51 cm.)

53

54

55

56

57

58

59

53
Unknown artist, Moscow, 1900s
Poster for mineral waters from the
Shabalovsky Factory of Karneyev,
Gorshanov & Co. Moscow.
43¼ × 31¼ in. (108 × 78 cm.)

54
Unknown artist, Moscow, no date
Label for table wine from the wholesale
warehouse of Semen Fedorovich Shlygin
of Tver.
5 × 3¾ in. (12.5 × 9.5 cm.)

55
Unknown artist, Moscow, no date
Label for a bottle of 'Russian Champagne
No. 48'. The manufacturer's name is
Viktor Vinogradov (*vinograd* is Russian
for grapes).
3¼ × 4¾ in. (8 × 12 cm.)

56
Unknown artist, no date
Label for a bottle of 'distilled wine' from
the firm of Vsevolod Karlovich
Donekovsky of Novocherkask.
3¼ × 2¾ in. (8 × 7 cm.)

57
Unknown artist, St. Petersburg, no date
Poster for 'synthetic lamp oil' from
the Libava Oil-Mill Company
(formerly Keeler).
21¼ × 12 in. (53 × 30 cm.)

58
Unknown artist, St. Petersburg, 1899
Poster: 'Look! Birch-balm for you from
Dr. Lengil of Vienna!'
22 × 9½ in. (55 × 24 cm.)

59
Unknown artist, St. Petersburg, no date
Label on a packet of cardboard tubes for
papirosi from L. Kaminer & Son, at their
Kharkov Mechanical Factory
3½ × 6 in. (9 × 15 cm.)

60

61

62

63

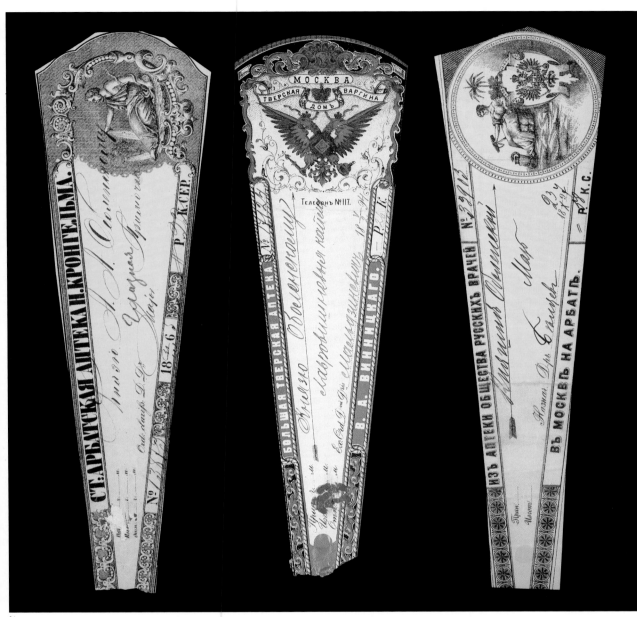

60
Unknown artist, Moscow, 1890s
Form from the firm of K. Blees & Co,
Moscow, a manufacturer of cloth and
worsted products.
11¼ × 8¾ in. (28 × 22 cm.)

61
Unknown artist, Moscow, no date
Detail of the cover of a wine-list. The
bottle label reads 'Green liqueur from
N.L. Shustov & Son'.

62
Unknown artist, Moscow, no date
Bottle label, reading 'Creme de Vanille
from the firm of Spiridon Nogin & Son in
the city of Ustyug'.
4½ × 3½ in. (11 × 8.5 cm.)

63
Unknown artist, Moscow, no date
Wine bottle label: 'Table wine No. 9 from
the V.A. Alexandrov distillery'.
4½ × 3½ in. (11 × 8.5 cm.)

64
Unknown artist, Moscow, second half of
nineteenth century
Pharmaceutical labels: Old Arbat
Pharmacy/N. Krongelm. Great Tver
Pharmacy. V.A. Vinnitsky. From the
Pharmacy of the Society of Russian
Doctors in Moscow, Arbat.
3½ × 10 in.; 3½ × 9¾ in.;
3 × 10½ in. (9 × 25 cm.;
8 × 24.5 cm.; 7.5 × 26 cm.)

65
Unknown artist, St. Petersburg, no date
Advertising card for the factory of A.N.
Shaposhnikov, St. Petersburg, showing a
box of papirosi.
3¼ × 5½ in. (8 × 13 cm.)

64

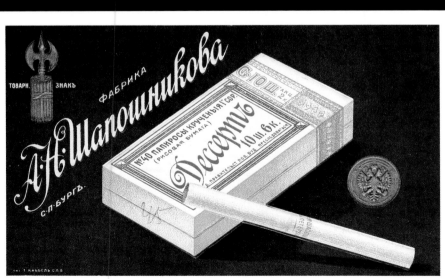

65

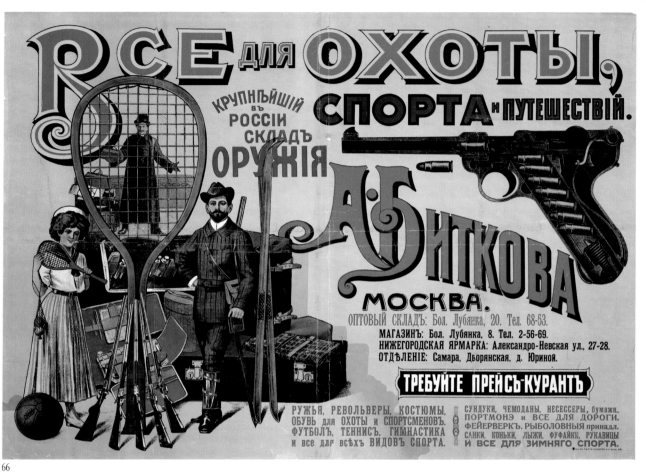

66

67

66
Unknown artist, Moscow, no date
Poster: 'Everything for hunting, sport and
travel. The largest selection of guns in
Russia – A. Bitkov, Moscow.'
32 × 42½ in. (80 × 106 cm.)

67
Unknown artist, St. Petersburg, 1899
Advertising poster for the firm of Starley.
16 × 42½ in. (40 × 106 cm.)

68
Unknown artist, St. Petersburg/Moscow,
no date
Polytype from the Leman type-foundry.

69
Unknown artist, Kiev, no date
Poster: 'All the latest equipment,
refinements and improvements for
aeroplanes and hydroplanes, from the
firm of Artur Anatr, Odessa. Construction
of aeroplanes to our own design or
any others'.
21¼ × 28½ in. (53 × 71 cm.)

70
Unknown artist, St. Petersburg, no date
Cover for *Vozdukhoplavaniye*
(aeronautics) chocolate, a product
from the firm of Krakhmalnikov
Brothers, Odessa.
4¾ × 9¼ in. (12 × 23 cm.)

69

70

71   71
                                                                 Unknown artist, Moscow, 1903
                                                                 Advertising leaflet: 'New! Royal
                                                                 Marmalade! A.I. Abrikosov & Sons,
                                                                 Moscow.
                                                                 14¾ × 9¼ in. (37 × 23 cm.)

                                                                 72
                                                                 F. Vendish, no date
                                                                 Poster for A.I. Abrikosov & Sons, Moscow.
                                                                 36½ × 16½ in. (91 × 41 cm.)

                                                                 73
                                                                 Unknown artist, no date
                                                                 Poster for *Utiniye Nosi* ('duck beak')
                                                                 sweets from A.I. Abrikosov & Sons,
                                                                 Moscow.
                                                                 29¼ × 14¾ in. (73 × 37 cm.)

72

73

74
Unknown artist, no date
Poster: 'Provodnik & Co. Galoshes.
10,000,000 pairs produced every
year. Unconditional guarantee of
complete reliability'.
40¾ × 27¼ in. (102 × 68 cm.)

75
Unknown artist, St. Petersburg, no da
Circular advertising leaflet for the
'Brewery of the House of P.P. Weiner'
in Astrakhan.
diameter 14 in. (35 cm.)

75

76
Unknown artist, St. Petersburg, no date
Poster for rubber sponges, a product
of Treugolnik.
19¼ × 12½ in. (48 × 31 cm.)

77
Unknown artist, St. Petersburg, no date
Poster for rubber toys from Treugolnik.
19¼ × 12½ in. (48 × 31 cm.)

78
Unknown artist, St. Petersburg, no date
Poster for rubber drive-belts for
agricultural purposes, from Treugolnik
19¼ × 12½ in. (48 × 31 cm.)

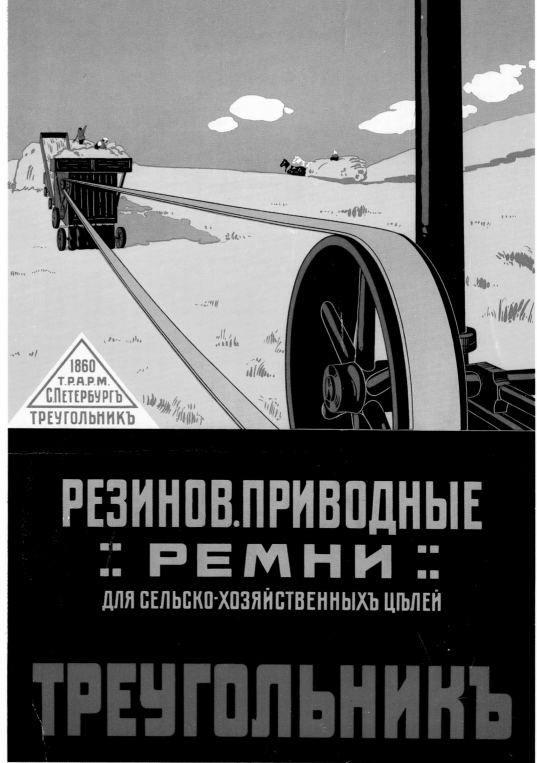

76

77

78

79

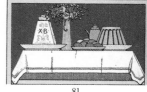

81

80

82

83

84
Unknown artist, St. Petersburg, no date
Poster advertising a blue soap for washing
clothes from the firm of A.M. Zhukov in
St. Petersburg.
21½ × 14½ in. (54 × 36 cm.)

85

85
Unknown artist, St. Petersburg, no date
The logo of A.M. Zhukov, based on the
word *zhuk*, or beetle.

86
Unknown artist, St. Petersburg, no date
Poster advertising soap and lamp oil from
A.M. Zhukov.
24¾ × 14 in. (62 × 35 cm.)

87
Unknown artist, St. Petersburg, no date
Poster 'A.M. Zhukov. Soap. St Petersburg.'
24 × 14½ in. (60 × 36 cm.)

88
Unknown artist (initials S.P.),
St. Petersburg, 1912
Poster: 'Five generations of experienced
housewives wash their clothes with
A.M. Zhukov's soap.'
14 × 20¼ in. (35 × 50.5 cm.)

86

87

88

90

89
Unknown artist, Moscow, 1903
Poster: 'Meller's Company. Moscow and
St. Petersburg. Representatives in
every town.'
33½ × 16 in. (84 × 40 cm.)

90
Unknown artist, Moscow, 1912
Poster: 'In the Kingdom of Gold', for
a charity bazaar and lottery in aid
of the poor.
55½ × 38 in. (139 × 95 cm.)

91
Unknown artist, no date
Poster: 'Kerosene burning street-lights
and lamps from the Lux Company of
Riga.' The caption to the picture
underneath reads 'The Tauride Palace in
St. Petersburg, lit by LUX lamps.'
29½ × 19¼ in. (74 × 48 cm.)

92
Unknown artist, St. Petersburg, 1905
Poster for the Russian–American Rubber
Manufacturing Company of
St Petersburg, showing life-size
cross sections of iron bands with
the appropriate rubber tyres.
19½ × 29¼ in. (49 × 73 cm.)

93
Unknown artist, Kiev, 1913
Poster: 'Karl Klein, Vilna. Manufacturer
of turbines, mills and tree-felling
machines. All equipment for mills
and saw-mills.' Parallel text in
Polish and Russian.
19¼ × 26 in. (48 × 65 cm.)

94
Unknown artist, St. Petersburg, no date
Poster: 'The Possel Works, St. Petersburg,
produce everything you need for
shoeing horses.'
16½ × 17¼ in. (41 × 43 cm.)

94

95

96

97

98

95
Unknown artist, St. Petersburg, no date.
Advertisement for Maltsov & Company.
'Traction-engines for agriculture
and industry.'
30¾ × 24 in. (77 × 60 cm.)

96
Unknown artist, St. Petersburg, no date
Poster for the Dresden Gas-Motor
Company: 'The cheapest form of energy.
Oil- and gas-powered generators.'
28¾ × 16 in. (72 × 40 cm.)

97
Unknown artist (initials M.F.), Moscow,
no date
Business card of the Mutual Society for
Insurance against Damage to Crops by
Hail (Moscow). Established in 1877
(detail).
4 × 6½ in. (10 × 16.5 cm.)

98/100
Unknown artist, St. Petersburg/Moscow,
no date
Polytypes from the Leman type-foundry.

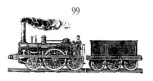

99

101
Unknown artist, Kiev, 1913
Poster: 'T. Yakobsen, Warsaw,
manufacturer of equipment for the
production of artificial mineral waters
and sparkling drinks.'
22 × 24 in (55 × 60 cm.)

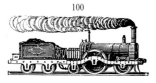

101

100

102

103

104

102
V. Pchelin, Moscow, 1910
Poster: 'TAP. The Automobile Transport Co. Hire of cars, open and closed carriages. Terms by taximeter or prior arrangement.'
14½ × 21¼ in. (36 × 53 cm.)

103
Unknown artist, St. Petersburg, no date
Poster: 'Nobel Bros. Oil, grease, petrol for cars, boats and aeroplanes.'
27¼ × 19½ in. (68.5 × 49 cm.)

104
N. Boutet, St. Petersburg, 1897
Menu design for a dinner arranged by the St. Petersburg River Yacht Club on 3 February 1897.

105
Unknown artist, St. Petersburg, no date
Poster: 'The Russia Rubber Factory. Proprietors: Freizinger Bros, Riga. Rubber tyres for bicycles, cars and carriages.'
27½ × 41¼ in. (69 × 103 cm.)

106
Unknown artist, Kiev, 1914
Poster advertising the sale and servicing of cars.
19½ × 21½ in. (49 × 54 cm.)

105

106

107
Unknown artist, St. Petersburg, 1903
Poster: 'Zoo, St. Petersburg, 1903'
36¾ × 27½ in. (92 × 69 cm.)

108
Unknown artist, St. Petersburg, no date
Poster: 'Everything for music. House of
L. Adler. Rostov-on-Don.'
20½ × 30 in. (51 × 75 cm.)

109
Unknown artist, St. Petersburg, no date
Poster: 'Thomas Alva Edison's greatest
invention. The kinetophone – singing and
talking movies.'
44½ × 29½ in. (111 × 74 cm.)

108

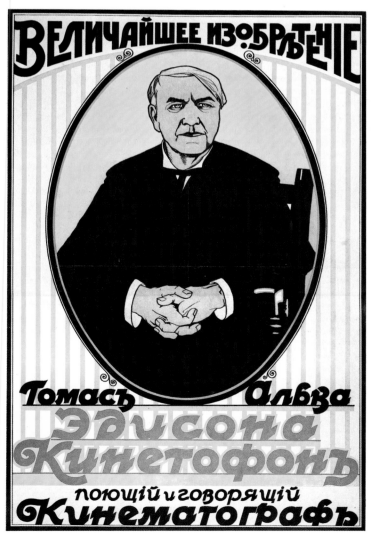

109

110

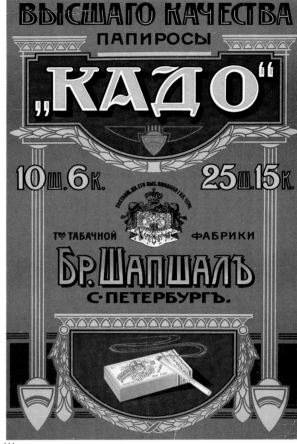

111

112

113

114

Ювелиръ
П. Вакъ
Существуетъ съ 1873 года
преемн. Г. О. Самуйлова,
Москва, Литейный 45-47.
ПОКУПАЮ
по высокимъ цѣнамъ дра-
гоцѣнные камни, бриллі-
анты, жемчугъ, ломбард-
ныя квитанціи.

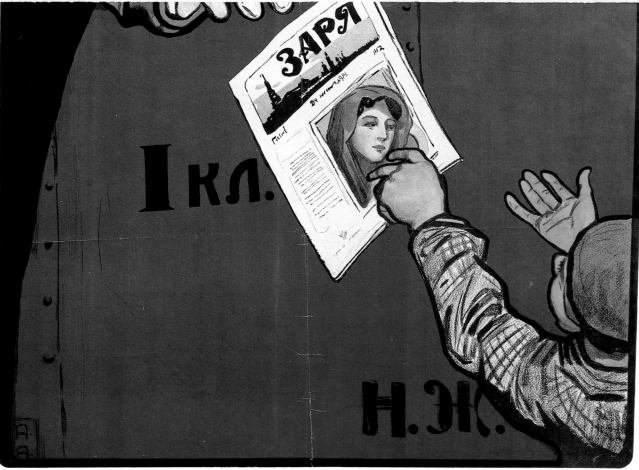

116

116
A. Apsit, Moscow, 1914
Poster advertising the journal *Zarya*
('Dawn')
44½ × 30 in. (111 × 75 cm.)

117
Unknown artist, St. Petersburg/Moscow,
no date
Polytype from the Leman type foundry.

118
Ye. Samokish-Sudkovskaya,
St. Petersburg
Poster advertising subscriptions to the art
and literary journal *Niva* ('Cornfield')
with literary supplements for the
year 1907.
44½ × 34 in. (111 × 85 cm.)

117

Е. САМОКИШ-СУДКОВСКАЯ.

НИВА ДАЕТЪ СВОИМЪ ПОДПИСЧИКАМЪ 1907 г.

52 №№ ХУДОЖЕСТВЕННО-ЛИТЕРАТУРНАГО ЖУРНАЛА „НИВА."
ПОЛНОЕ СОБРАНІЕ СОЧИНЕНІЙ въ

10 КНИ-ГАХЪ ГР. А. К. ТОЛСТОГО.

ОСТАЛЬНЫЯ 30 КНИГЪ полнаго собранія сочиненій К. М. СТАНЮКОВИЧА.

12 КНИГЪ Ежемѣсячныхъ литературныхъ и популярно-научныхъ Приложеній.

Всего 52 книги, т. е. по одной книгѣ при каждомъ № „НИВЫ".

12 №№ „ПАРИЖСКИХЪ МОДЪ" До 200 столбцовъ текста, со множествомъ иллюстрацій и почтовыхъ ящиковъ для отвѣтовъ на разнообразные вопросы подписчиковъ.

12 ЛИСТОВЪ рукодѣльныхъ, ажурныхъ и выпильн. работъ и чертежей выкроекъ.

1 СТѢННОЙ КАЛЕНДАРЬ на 1907 годъ, отпечатанный въ 10 красокъ по акварели Е. П. Самокишъ-Судковской.

ОТКРЫТА ПОДПИСКА на „НИВУ" 1907 года.

Подписная цѣна на годовое изданіе „НИВЫ" 1907 года со всѣми приложеніями:

Безъ доставки въ С.-Петербургѣ **6 р. 50 к.**	Безъ доставки въ Москвѣ въ конторѣ Н. ПЕЧКОВСКОЙ (Петровскія линіи) **7 р. 25 к.**	
Съ доставкою въ С.-Петербургѣ **7 р. 50 к.**	Безъ доставки въ Одессѣ въ кн. маг. „ОБРАЗОВАНІЕ" (Ришельевская, 12). **7 р. 50 к.**	
Съ пересылкою во всѣ города и мѣстности Россіи **8 р.**	Съ пересылкой за границу **12 р.**	

Новые подписчики на 1907 г., желающіе получить **ПЕРВЫЯ 10 КНИГЪ** сочиненій **К. М. СТАНЮКОВИЧА,** доплачиваютъ:

Безъ доставки въ С.-Петербургѣ **1 р. 50 к.**	Безъ доставки въ Москвѣ и Одессѣ **1 р. 75 к.**	Съ дост. въ Спб. и перес. иногородн. и за границу **2 р.**

Подписка принимается въ Главной Конторѣ журнала „НИВА", С.-Петербургъ, ул. Гоголя, 22.

119

119
Unknown artist, St Petersburg, no date
Poster: 'Only BROM *papirosi* calm the
nerves, thanks to a special selection of
Turkish tobacco. The Crimean Tobacco
Factory Co.'
20 × 13¼ in. (50 × 33 cm.)

120
Unknown artist, St. Petersburg/Moscow,
no date
Polytype from the Leman type-foundry.

121
Unknown artist, St. Petersburg, no date
Poster: 'New! Fantastic! *Duchesse*
tobacco. The Kolobov and Bobrov
Tobacco Factory.'
56 × 47¼ in. (140 × 118 cm.)

122
Unknown artist, no date
Poster: 'I. Isadzhanov's cardboard
tubes for *papirosi*. Moscow.
Flexible mouthpieces'
28½ × 14½ in. (71 × 36 cm.)

123
Unknown artist, no date
Poster: 'Smoke Kalf Bros.
(Kharkov) *papirosi*.'
28 × 14 in. (70 × 35 cm.)

124
Unknown artist, St. Petersburg, 1912
Poster advertising *Roskosh* ('luxury') and
Tari-Bari 'tittle-tattle') *papirosi* from the
Shaposhnikov and Co. Tobacco Factory,
St. Petersburg.
28½ × 15½ in. (71 × 38.5 cm.)

120

121

122

123

124

На
Помощь
Жертвамъ
войны

ВЫСТАВКА
КАРТИНЪ И СКУЛЬПТУРЬ

2

5

POLITICAL GRAPHICS

The first day of August 1914 saw the German declaration of war on Russia.

The poster entitled 'Aid for the Victims of War' with which this chapter opens was commissioned several days later. On the day designated for the collection of donations the poster was displayed all over Moscow. As the artist, Leonid Pasternak, recalled: 'Crowds stood before the poster, old women wept... The collection was handled by many famous theatre artists, headed by Sobinov. Postcards of my "Wounded Soldier", printed in tens and hundreds of thousands, were sold at high prices... The excellent English journal *Studio* also reproduced "Soldier". In a word, the success of the work exceeded all expectations. Pirate editions of the poster appeared on chocolate wrappers, labels and even trademarks.'[26]

Immediately following the outbreak of war artists became furiously engaged in charitable activities. They organized numerous exhibitions, the proceeds of which went to aid war victims and their families. Posters for every kind of war charity were produced by great Russian artists such as Victor Vasnetsov and Konstantin Korovin. One such invited the public to a charity bazaar (fig. 36), another announced an appeal on behalf of the 'All-Russian Union of Zemstvos in aid of the sick and wounded' to donate clothing and food to the wounded, widows and orphans.

The other main theme dominating posters during the war years was the drive to encourage the public to buy war bonds. Slogans such as 'Hasten victory over the enemy!' and 'Fight to the finish!' drummed the message home. In fact Russia was to cover two-thirds of its war expenditure by the sale of war bonds within the Empire.

In addition to posters the graphic art of the war years included postcards, book-covers and magazine illustrations, produced by artists of various ages, abilities and artistic persuasions; all of them, however, encountering the genre of political graphics for the first time. They were obliged to develop their own approaches to the new themes and challenges provided by the war with only their individual artistic experience to guide them.

Pasternak, a graphic artist of the academic school, drew his famous poster from life; a soldier in full battle-dress was sent to pose for him. Artists working in the Neo-Russian style made use of the legendary Bogatyrs and the figures of Russian field-marshals in their treatment of patriotic themes;

they evoked past glories and famous victories of Russian history and also incorporated some elements of the national decorative tradition. Narbut, for example, frequently employed heraldic motifs. Many artists turned to the idiom of popular prints *(luboks)*, which served, for the simple and illiterate as a chronicle of military events, expecially in the early days of the war. As a rule, these prints were hastily produced, rather crude illustrations; but there were exceptions, some of which are reproduced here.

The most interesting appeared under the imprint of Lubok Today, a publishing house set up immediately after the outbreak of war which employed the services of some excellent artists. Especially noteworthy is a series of prints commissioned by the publishers from Kazimir Malevich and Vladimir Mayakovsky. The series was singled out by critics as the best work in an exhibition entitled 'War and Printing', staged in Petrograd in late 1914. 'The most amusing series of Lubok Today and probably the most inventive and boldly decorative in its use of colour comes from the brush of the Moscow Futurists.'[27] The Futurists, as all artists belonging to the growing Russian avant garde movement were then collectively known, were the better able to understand and develop the *lubok* tradition because they were the first to explore and appreciate the unique artistic world of popular painting – the *lubok*, shop and inn signs and so on. The success of Lubok Today was short-lived, however, and all the work reproduced in this book dates from the year 1914. The reality of war – 'The horror of war came very close', in Mayakovsky's words – rendered the 'amusing' character of its publications increasingly inappropriate, especially as the full potential of documentary photography, which gradually earned the public's confidence, became apparent.

3

3
N.I. Piskarev, 1914
Poster for the exhibition of pictures and sculpture: 'Moscow Artists for Victims of the War' (detail). The poster was published in various formats.
46 × 29½ in. (115 × 74 cm.)

4/5
Unknown artist, Kiev, 1916
Form-letters for illiterate soldiers to send home from the front, a series. They open with 'My dear, gentle little wife' or 'My dear sweet-heart'. Text under illustrations: 'In the bosom of the family' and 'Well, dearest, goodbye, write often and don't forget me!'
7¼ × 4¾ in. (18 × 12 cm.)

Some of the following posters include 'text in verse' by Vladimir Mayakovsky. The verses are deliberately crude – even brutal – doggerel; their purpose was to raise the spirits of dispirited soldiers fighting in the appalling conditions of the First World War.

6
Vladimir Mayakovsky, 1914 (?)
Lubok (popular print, detail). The text is also by Mayakovsky:
'At Warsaw and Grodno we thrashed 'em, Yes, we thrashed the Germans and smashed 'em''

Среди родной семьи.

Дорогая, любезная моя женушка!

Прежде всего спѣшу увѣдомить тебя, что я, слава Богу, живъ и здоровъ, чего и тебѣ отъ души желаю.
Постоянно вспоминаю о тебѣ и о всей нашей дорогой семьѣ, съ нетерпѣніемъ постоянно жду отъ тебя вѣстей, а получаю твои письма съ великою радостью, прочитываю ихъ по много разъ и какъ будто-бы вижу Васъ всѣхъ въ это время, моихъ дорогихъ, возлѣ себя и бесѣдую съ Вами.
Поэтому прошу тебя, моя дорогая, пиши

4

Ну! дорогая, прощай, почаще пиши и меня не забывай!

Дорогая моя возлюбленная!

Спѣшу увѣдомить тебя, моя дорогая, что я, слава Богу, живъ и здоровъ, чего и тебѣ отъ души желаю.
Часто я и въ тяжелыхъ и радостныхъ случаяхъ моей военной жизни вспоминаю о тебѣ, моя дорогая, о твоей любви и ласкахъ, о проведенномъ съ тобою счастливомъ времени и утѣшаюсь мыслью, что ты тамъ обо мнѣ не забываешь.

5

6

Ну и трескъ-же, ну и громъ-же
Былъ отъ нѣмцевъ подлѣ Ломжи!

8

7
Kazimir Malevich, 1914 (?)
Lubok, verse by Mayakovsky:
'At Lomzhe, when we beat the Kraut
All he did was scream and shout.'
15¼ × 22½ in. (38 × 56 cm.)

8
I. Mashkov, 1914 (?)
Detail of a *lubok*.

9
Kazimir Malevich, 1914 (?)
Lubok, verse by Mayakovsky:
'The French filled their mushroom
baskets with Huns.
While Tommies filled tubs with Kraut
fathers and sons!'
16 × 23¼ in. (40 × 58 cm.)

10
Kazimir Malevich, 1914 (?)
Lubok: 'Kaiser Bill's Roundabout'. Verse
by Mayakovsky:
'Near Paris they gave us a good hard
lickin'
While I ran round like a headless
chicken!'
15¼ × 22½ in. (38 × 56 cm.)

У союзниковъ французовъ
Битыхъ нѣмцевъ полный кузовъ,

А у братцевъ англичанъ
Драныхъ нѣмцевъ цѣлый чанъ.

9

ВИЛЬГЕЛЬМОВА КАРУСЕЛЬ.

„Подъ Парижемъ на краю
Лупятъ армію мою,

А я кругомъ бѣгаю
Да ничего не сдѣлаю".

10

Глядь, поглядь, ужъ близко Вислы
Нѣмцевъ пучитъ, значитъ кисло!

Типо-Литографія С. М. Мухарскаго, Москва.

Издательство „СЕГОДНЯШНІЙ ЛУБОКЪ" Москва, Тверская, 29, кв. 30. Тел. 2-78-84.

12

11
Kazimir Malevich, 1914 (?)
Lubok, verse by Mayakovsky:
'At Vissla the Germans cursed their luck,
And then, by God, they ran amok!'
22½ × 15¼ in. (56 × 38 cm.)

12
I. Mashkov, 1914 (?)
Detail of a *lubok*.

13
Kazimir Malevich, 1914 (?)
Lubok, verse by Mayakovsky:
'An Austrian thought he'd rule over the
Poles
But a farm-girl's pitchfork filled his arse
full of holes!'

14
Kazimir Malevich, 1914 (?)
Lubok, verse by Mayakovsky:
'When the Germans came to Lodz
We had to bow before the sods
But when they tried the same at Raad
We kicked their arses good and hard!'
15¼ × 22¾ in. (38 × 57 cm.)

Шелъ австріецъ въ Радзивилы,
Да попалъ на бабьи вилы.

13

Подошелъ колбасникъ къ Лодзи   Ну, а съ Лодзью рядомъ Радомъ
Мы сказали: „Панъ добродзи!"   И ушелъ съ подбитымъ задомъ.

14

Нѣмецъ рыжій и шершавый   Да казакъ Данило Дикій   И ему жена Полина
Разлетался надъ Варшавой,   Продырявилъ его пикой   Шьетъ штаны изъ цепелина.

15

Австрійни у Карпатъ,   Гнали всю Галицію,
Поднимали благой матъ.   Шайку глуполицую.

16

17

15
Kazimir Malevich, 1914 (?)
Lubok, verse by Mayakovsky:
'A hairy German in
His great big Zeppelin
Was cruising over Warsaw without fear,
Till a Cossack, Dan the Wild
Kissed his wife, Polina, smiled,
Reached up and punctured it – with just
his spear!
Then clever young Polina
Cut up the "Zeppelina"
For trousers – just to cover Danny's rear!'

16
Vladimir Mayakovsky, 1914 (?)
Lubok, text in verse by Mayakovsky:
'The Austrians in Carpathia?
For help they had to shout!
The Austrians in Galicia?
We chased the bugggers out!'
15½ × 22¼ in. (38.5 × 55.5 cm.)

17
I. Mashkov, 1914 (?)
Detail of a *lubok*.

18
Vladimir Mayakovsky, 1914 (?)
Lubok, text in verse by Mayakovsky:
'You'll never get to Paris, Fritz,
Though you fight through thick and thin!
And *if* you get to Paris, Fritz,
We'll be in Berlin!'
15¼ × 22½ in. (38 × 56 cm.)

19
Vladimir Mayakovsky, 1914 (?)
Lubok, verse by Mayakovsky:
'If you'd stayed at home to tend your
roses
We wouldn't have given you bloody
noses!'
(Addressed to the Ottoman Turks.)
15¼ × 22½ in. (38 × 56 cm.)

Эхъ ты нѣмецъ, при да при же
Не допрешь, чтобъ сѣсть въ Парижѣ

И ужъ братецъ—клиномъ клинъ:
Ты въ Парижъ, а мы въ Берлинъ!

18

Эхъ султанъ сидѣлъ бы въ Портѣ,
Дракой рыла не попорти.

19

Масса нѣмцевъ пѣшихъ, конныхъ   Да казаки по опушкѣ   И подъ—лихъ казачій гомонъ—
Ѣдутъ съ пушками въ вагонахъ,   Раскидали нѣмцамъ пушки   Вражій поѣздъ былъ изломанъ!

20

КАЗАКЪ И НѢМЦЫ.

21

22

20
A. Lentulov, 1914 (?)
Lubok
'A load of Huns
With artillery guns
Tried to protect their train.
But the Cossacks attacked
The train was sacked
And the cannon went down the drain!'
15¼ × 22 in. (38 × 55 cm.)

21
Georgi Narbut, 1914 (?)
Lubok: 'The Cossack and the Germans'
16½ × 22¾ in. (41 × 57 cm.)

22
I. Mashkov, 1914 (?)
Detail of a *lubok*.

23
Dimitri Moor, 1914 (?)
Lubok: 'The heroic deed of Kozma
Kryuchkov the Bogatyr'. 'Four Cossacks –
Kozma Kryuchkov, Astakhov, Ivankov and
Shchekolkov – chased 27 German
cavalrymen and challenged them to
fight. Kozma bayonetted 11 of them; he
was wounded 16 times and his horse 11
times.' For this act of heroism Kozma
received the Cross of St. George with
ribbon. The picture shows a gigantic
Kozma spearing Germans and planting
them like trees. 'A forest like that makes
the way home a bit cooler!'
16¾ × 23¼ in. (42 × 58 cm.)

24
Dimitri Moor, 1914–1916
Lubok, 'How the Devil kicked up a fuss.'
16 × 23¼ in. (40 × 58 cm.)

23

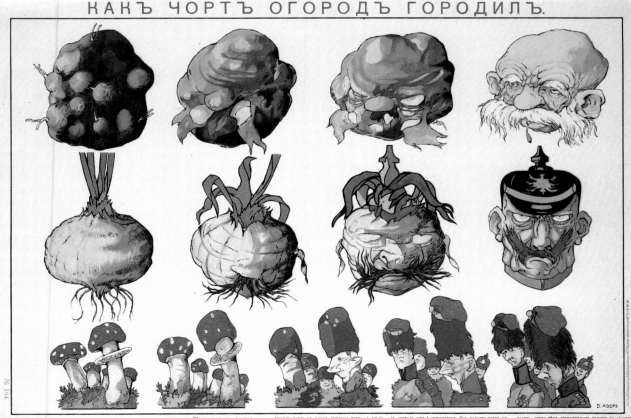

24

Нѣмцы! Сильны хоша вы,   Лучше бы въ Берлинъ поперли
А не видѣть вамъ Варшавы   Всѣ пока не перемерли.

25

Въ славномъ лѣсѣ Августовомъ   Врагъ изрубленъ, а затѣмъ онъ
Битыхъ нѣмцевъ тысячъ сто вамъ   Пущенъ плавать въ синій Нѣманъ.

25

Kazimir Malevich (?), 1914 (?)
Lubok, verse by Mayakovsky:
'You'll never see Warsaw, you Germans
However hard you try!
Stay in Berlin, you Germans,
Unless you want to die!'
15¼ × 22½ in. (38 × 56 cm.)

26

Vladimir Mayakovsky, 1914 (?)
Lubok, verse by Mayakovsky:
'Near the lovely, lovely forest of Augustus
We killed a hundred thousand Germans
dead.
And the River Neman's dark, dark blue
waters
Ran red, red, red.'
15¼ × 22½ in. (38 × 56 cm.)

27

27
L. Goranlovsky, 1914
Poster: 'Donate your dolls for
war-orphans.'
24¾ × 13½ in. (62 × 34 cm.)

28
Unknown artist, no date
Wrapper for *Poteshnïye* ('boy-soldiers',
from a regiment of boy-soldiers formed
by Peter the Great). One of a series.
The theme of this drawing is
'the orderly's report'.

29
A. Krasovsky, 1915
Easter card.
3½ × 5¾ in. (9 × 14.5 cm.)

30/31
A. Krasovsky (?), 1915
Easter cards
Both, 3½ × 5¾ in. (9 × 14.5 cm.)

ВСЕРОССІЙСКІЙ ЗЕМСКІЙ СОЮЗЪ

ПОМОЩИ БОЛЬНЫМЪ И РАНЕНЫМЪ.

СОСТОЯЩІЙ ПОДЪ ПОКРОВИТЕЛЬСТВОМЪ

ЕЯ ИМПЕРАТОРСКАГО ВЫСОЧЕСТВА

ВЕЛИКОЙ КНЯГИНИ

ЕЛИСАВЕТЫ ѲЕОДОРОВНЫ

СБОРЪ МОСКОВСКАГО

ГУБЕРНСКАГО КОМИТЕТА.

ЖЕРТВУЙТЕ

ТЕПЛУЮ ОДЕЖДУ, НОСИЛЬ-
НОЕ ПЛАТЬЕ, БѢЛЬЕ, ОБУВЬ,
ПИЩЕВЫЕ ПРОДУКТЫ

РАНЕНЫМЪ,

ПО ВЫЗДОРОВЛЕНІИ ОТПРА-
ВЛЯЕМЫМЪ НА СВОЕ ЖИ-
ТЕЛЬСТВО, И НУЖДАЮЩИМ-
СЯ СЕМЬЯМЪ ЗАПАСНЫХЪ—
ВДОВАМЪ И СИРОТАМЪ.
ПРИГОТОВЬТЕ ВАШИ
ПОЖЕРТВОВАНІЯ,
МЫ ПРІѢДЕМЪ ЗА
НИМИ.

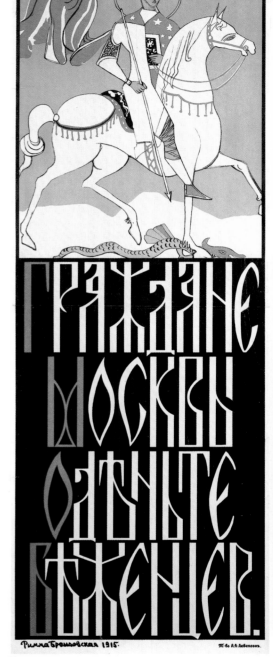

34

32
K. Korovin, 1914
Poster requesting the donation of clothes,
food, etc for war-wounded, widows and
orphans. Text round the picture: 'Give to
those who gave all in war. Dmitry
Donskoi, 1380–1914'.
49¾ × 36¾ in. (124.5 × 92 cm.)

33
R. Braillovskaya, 1915
Poster: 'Citizens of Moscow, donate
clothes for refugees!'
56 × 16½ in. (140 × 41 cm.)

34/35
Kozlov, 1915
Details of a programme cover for an
evening of Russian music. The theme
of the evening was 'Students for the
Defense of Russia.'

36
Victor Vasnetsov, 1914
Poster: '5, 6 and 7 December 1914.
Charity bazaar in all rooms of the
Assembly of the Russian Nobility
in aid of war victims.'
49½ × 37¼ in. (124 × 93 cm.)

35

36

38

37
Boris Kustodiev, 1917
Poster: 'Freedom bonds!'
40¼ × 27¼ in. (100.5 × 68 cm.)

38
Unknown artist, no date
Drawing on notepaper.

39
Unknown artist, Petrograd, 1916
Poster: 'War bonds – 5%. Purpose of
loan: to hasten victory over the enemy.'
26¾ × 40 in. (67 × 100 cm.)

40
Unknown artist, 1916
Poster for the 5% war bond.
28 × 40¾ in. (70 × 102 cm.)

37

39

40

1   Konstantin S. Stanislavsky: *Moya zhizn v iskusstve,* Moscow, Iskusstvo, 1980: 28

2   *'Pechatnoye iskusstvo',* October 1901: 27

3   *'Iskusstvo i khudozhestvennaya promyshlennost',* no.8, 1899: 681

4   *Khronika zhurnala, 'Iskusstvo i khudozhestvennaya promyshlennost',* no.6, 1899-1900: 143

5   *Alexandre Benois razmyshlyaet…,* Moscow, Sovietskii Khudozhnik, 1968: 613

6   *'Iskusstvo i khudozhestvennaya promyshlennost',* no. 7, 1899: 609

7   *'Mir iskusstva',* nos. 21-22, 1899: 35

8   V. I. Butovsky: *Istoria russkogo ornamenta s X do XVI stoletiye po drevnym rukopisyam,* Moscow, 1870: 1

9   Vasily V. Stasov: *Slavyanskii i vostochniy ornament po rukopisyam drevnogo i novogo vremeni,* St. Petersburg, 1887, unpaginated.

10 Konstantin S. Stanislavsky: *Moya zhizn v iskusstve,* Moscow, Iskusstvo, 1980: 187

11 *Sovremennaya russkaya grafika* (redaktsia, Sergei Makovsky, text, N. Radlova), St. Petersburg, 1917: XIV

12 *Ibid.:* XVII

13 *Obzor pervoi vcerossiiskoi vystavki pechatnogo dela,* St. Petersburg, no.1, 1895: 2

14 *Ibid.:* no.16: 5

15 *Ibid.:* no.21: 3

16 *Vystavka prouzvedenii pechati za 1909 goda,* St. Petersburg, 1911: 1

17 *'Iskusstvo i khudozhestvennaya promyshlennost',* no.7, 1899: 610

18 *Ibid.*

19 *Ibid.:* no.8, 1899: 689

20 *Ibid.,* no.7, 1899: 611

21 *Ibid.:* 612

22 *Ibid.:* 611

23 *'Pechatnoye iskusstvo',* no.1, 1901: 1

24 P. Kolomnin: *Veseda o nabore titulov i yeshcho koye o chem drugom,* St. Petersburg, 1914: 3

25 Leonid O. Pasternak: *Zapisi raznikh let,* Moscow, 1975: 89

26 G. Magula: *Voina i narodniye kartini, 'Lukomoriye',* no.30, 1914: 17

Abramtsevo 20, 68
advertising cards *99, 111*
advertising leaflets *114, 116*
All-Russian Congress of Artists (1911) 9-10
Apollon 71, 80, 82
Apsit, A.: advertising poster *134*
Art and Industrial Design 10-12, 16, 88-90, 91
Art Nouveau 39, 43, 44
Art Nouveau, Russian *see moderne* style
Art of Printing, The 90

Bakhrushin, Alexei 7
Bakst, Lev (Léon) 65, 67, 69, 70, 76
　book cover *78*
　card ('My Favourite Poet') *76*
　cover for *World of Art* 65
　frontispiece to *The Snow Mask* 76
　illustration for *Sliyaniye* 76
　posters *76,78*
　theatre programme cover *84*
　vignettes *76*
Balmont, K.
　'Hymn to the Sun' *81*
　The Fire-Bird 74
　Sliyaniye ('Confluence') *76*
banknotes *87, 89, 90, 93*
Beardsley, Aubrey 68
Belinsky, Vissarion 15
Belsky, M. (?)
　perfume labels *59, 61*
　soap wrappers *40, 41, 43, 45, 59*
Belzen, Ya. Ya.: poster *53*
Bem, Yelizaveta 16
Benois, Alexandre 11, 12, 65, 67, 69, 70, 75
　cards ('Easter in the XVIII Century') *75*
　illustrations for *The Queen of Spades* 75
　menu *27*
　silhouette *74*
　Tsarskoe Selo 81
　vignettes for 'Florence' *66*
　vignette from *Golden Fleece* 69
Benois, Nikolai 65
Berthold & Co. 6, 90
Bilibin, Ivan 16, 67, 69
　illumination for 'Maria Morevna' *19*
　illumination for 'Vasilisa the Magnificent' *15*
　illustration for 'The Tale of the Fisherman and the Fish' *21*
　illustrations for 'The Tale of Tsar Saltan' *16, 19*
　initial vignettes for *Golden Fleece* 32, 35, 37
　posters *32*
Blok, Alexander: *The Snow Mask* 76
bottle labels *106, 109, 111*
Boutet, N.: menu design *128*
Braillovskaya, R.: poster *155*
Burnovo, A.: posters *35, 37*
Butovsky: *History of Russian Ornamental Design . . .* 18-19

Chekhonin, Sergei 70
　type-face initial *84*
Chekhov, Anton 43; *The Seagull* 43
Chernyshevsky, Nikolai 15
chocolate wrappers *21, 22, 25, 27, 53, 100, 103, 105, 112*
cigarette packets *see papirosi*
Community of St Eugenia of the Red Cross 12
　envelopes *84*
　postcards *72, 75, 76*
　writing paper *79*

Dalmatov, K.: embroidery collection 87
Diaghilev, Sergei 16, 65-6, 67, 70
Dobrolyubov, Nikolai 15
Dobuzhinsky, Mstislav 65, 67, 79

book covers *79*
　colophon from *Golden Fleece* 79
　invitation card cover *79*
　programme cover *79*
　silhouette *79*
　vignette from *World of Art* 69

Easter cards *99, 153*
envelopes 11-12, *84*
'Exhibitions of the Printed Word' (1908-13) 88

Filosofov, Dmitri 65
Firsov, Ye.: poster *35*
First All-Russian Printing Exhibition (1895) 87, 88
form-letters *141*
Futurists, the 140

Gartman, Viktor 18
Gerardov, N.N.: poster *51*
Golden Fleece: colophon *79*; vignettes *32, 35, 37, 69, 76*
Golovin, A.: theatre programme covers *84*
Goranlovsky, L.: poster *153*
Grabar, I.: *History of Russian Art* 80

Hamsun, Knut 79

International Exhibition of Art Posters (1897) 9
International Photographic Exhibitions (1903, 1908) 91
Isenberg, K.V.: poster *57*
Ivanov, Vyacheslav: *Cor Ardens* 72

Kalmakov, N.: illustration for book plate *47*
Kekusheva, Ya.: poster *53*
Kiseleva, E.: poster *39*
Klimenko, V.: Easter card *99*
Korovin, K.: poster *155*
Kozlov: programme cover *155*
Kramskoi, Ivan 16
Krasnov, N.: menu *22*
Krasovsky, A.: Easter cards *153*
Krylov: *Fables* 82, 83
Kustodiev, Boris: poster *156*

labels: perfume *59, 61*; wine *106, 109, 111*
Lansere, Yevgeny 65, 69, 80
　cover for *World of Art* 65
　illustration for Balmont's 'Hymn to the Sun' *81*
　illustration from Benois *Tsarskoe Selo* 81
　logo for Exhibitions of Contemporary Art 80
　poster *81*
　vignette from *History of Russian Art* 80
Leman, Ivan 90
Leman type-foundry *28, 54, 61, 90, 94, 99, 112, 127, 133, 134, 136*
Lentulov, A.: *lubok 149*
Levitsky, Dmitri 70
Livre de la Marquise, Le 71, 74
luboks (prints) 140, *141, 143, 145, 147, 149, 151*
Lubok Today 140

Makovsky, Sergei 68
Makovsky, Vladimir 16
Malevich, Kazimir: *luboks* (prints) 140, *143, 145, 147, 151*
Mamontov, Savva Ivanovich 8, 20, 66
Marx, Adolf 8
Mashkov, I.: *luboks 143, 145, 147, 149*
Mayakovsky, Vladimir: *luboks* (prints) 140, *141, 147, 151*
menu illustrations *15, 21, 22, 25, 27, 30*
Mitrokhin, Dimitri 70
moderne Buchschmuck in Russland, Der 70
moderne style 9, 39-44
Moor, Dimitri: *luboks 149*
Morozov, Ivan 7

Morozov, Sergei 7, 40
Moscow: shopping streets 7, *8*
Moscow Art Theatre for All 40-2, 43
Mucha, Alphonse 43

Narbut, Georgi 70, 82, 140
　book illustrations *82, 83*
　envelopes for visiting cards *84*
　lubok ('The Cossack and the Germans') *149*
　title pages *82, 83*
　vignettes *82*
Nemirovich-Danchenko, Vladimir 40
Neo-Russian Style, the 20, 139-40
Nevinsky, I.: menu *25*
New Satiricon 80
Niva 8, 87, *134*
Nizhny Novgorod Trade Fair 92
Nuvel, Walter 65

Ostashov, P.: advertisement *93*
Ostroumova-Lebedeva, A. 69
　engraving from 'Views of St Petersburg' *69*

papirosi packets *57, 100, 103, 105, 109*
Paramonov, A.: poster *37*
Pashkov, G.P.: poster *139*
Pasternak, Leonid 139-40
　poster 139, *139*
Pchelin, V.: poster *128*
perfume labels *59, 61*
pharmaceutical labels *111*
Pisarev, Dimitrii 15
Piskarev, N.I.: poster *141*
polytypes *54, 61, 94, 99, 112, 127, 134, 136*
Ponomarenko, Ya.: poster *53*
postcards 11-12, 16, *72, 75, 76*
posters 9, 91
　advertising balls *39, 45, 49, 51*
　advertising exhibitions *35, 37, 53, 57, 76, 81, 139, 141*
　advertising film and theatre *47*
　advertising war bonds *156*
　announcement *28*
　campaign against tuberculosis *54*
　charity *78, 99*
　commercial *32, 57, 61, 88, 93-136*
　war 139-40, *153, 155*
printing processes, development of 90-1
prints, popular *see luboks*
Prodberesky, N.: poster *51*
programmes, theatre and concert *27, 30, 72, 79, 84, 155*
Prokhorov, Alexei 7
Pushkin, Aleksandr 69
　The Queen of Spades 75

Remizov, Alexei 79
Remizov, Nikolai 80
　posters *80, 81*
Repin, Ilya 16
Review of the First All-Russian Printing Exhibition 87
Ropet, Ivan 19, 87
　Coronation announcement *28*
'Russian Style', the 17-19, 87
　typeface *28*

St Petersburg: Apraksin Dvor *12*;
　Nevsky Prospekt *10*
Samokish Sudkovskaya, Ye.: advertising poster *134*
Satiricon 80
Serov, Valentin 69
Shabelskaya, N. 11
Shchukin, Sergei 7
Shekhtel, Fyodor 40, 41, 43

Singer Sewing Machine Co. *10, 96*
soap wrappers *40, 41, 43, 45, 59, 103*
Somov, Konstantin 6, 65, 67, 69, 70, 71, 91
    book cover (*Cor Ardens*) *72*
    book cover (*The Fire-Bird*) *74*
    illustrations from *Le Livre de la Marquise 71, 74*
    'The Kiss' (silhouette) *71*
    silhouette *72*
    theatre programme covers *72*
    title page from *Theatre 71*
    vignettes from postcards *72*
Somov, Sergei 65
Stanislavsky, Konstantin 8, 40, 41
Stasov, Vasily 16, 18, 19
    Slav and Eastern Ornamental Design ... 19
Stepanov, Ivan 12
style Russe see 'Russian Style', the
sweet wrappers *61, 63*

(*see also* chocolate wrappers)
Sytin, Ivan D. 8

Talashkino 20, 68
Telyakovsky: poster *49*
Tenisheva, Princess Maria 20, 66
Tretyakov, Pavel 7

Vasnetsov, Victor 11, 12, 19-20, 41, *94*
    menus *15, 21, 22, 25, 27*
    poster *155*
    Three Bogatyrs 68
Vassilyev, N.: poster *49*
Vendish, F.: poster *114*
vignettes *35, 37, 66* 68, *69, 72, 76, 80, 82*
Vrubel, Mikhail 41, 69
    poster *37*

Vysheslavtsev, N.: poster *47*

Wanderers, the (*peredvishniki*) 16, 19
wine labels *106, 109, 111*
World Exposition, Paris (1900) 39, 69
World of Art 6, 10-11, 12, 16, 65, 66, 67, 68-9. 70, *81*, 91; covers *65*;
    vignettes *66, 69, 76*
World of Art group 13, 65-70, 91

Yaguzhinsky, S.: menus *25, 30*

Zakharov, F.: poster *54*
Zvorykin, B.
    advertising poster *133*
    menu *27*
    programme for reception *27*
    theatre and concert programmes *30*